The California Native
Copper Canyon
Companion

The California Native International Adventures

WELCOME to our California Native Copper Canyon Adventure. The Sierra Madre Mountains of northern Mexico encompass a vast scenic area of pine forested mountains cleaved by deep canyons. This is the homeland of the Tarahumara Indians, the world's greatest long-distance runners, who still practice their ancient traditional lifestyle, living in caves and simple shelters.

The Chihuahua al Pacifico Railroad, which traverses the area, has been called one of the most spectacular train rides in the Western Hemisphere.

For two decades, we have been operating the very best trips through Copper Canyon. Our guides are known throughout the area for their work with the Tarahumaras and we have become a major source of information on this remote area of Mexico.

To make your trip more enjoyable we have prepared this book written by members of our California Native staff.

Contents

Albert Kimsey Owen, at left, with other leaders of his colony, in 1886 founded a utopian community at Mexico's Topolobampo Bay, gateway to Copper Canyon, and created the spectacular Copper Canyon Railroad.

Topolobampo or Bust

By Don Fuchik

In 1874, Commander George Dewey sailed the United States sloop-of-war Narragansett into Mexico's Topolobampo Bay. This was the same George Dewey who, 25 years later, defeated the Spanish Navy at Manila Bay after giving his famous command, "You may fire when you are ready, Gridley."

The mission into Topolobampo was a peaceful one; its goal was to survey the Pacific Coast of Mexico and Baja California. The survey was ordered by President Grant at the behest of Albert Kimsey Owen, a former railroad surveyor and city planner, who had grandiose plans to develop a great harbor at Topolobampo.

The harbor was only part of his plans. A railroad would be built from Topolobampo through Mexico and the United States to the Atlantic Ocean, facilitating trade between Europe, the United States, and the Far East. In addition, the area around Topolobampo would be populated with a utopian American colony.

Owen entered into an agreement to purchase 111,000 acres from a local hacienda owner and, with the help of Mexican president Porfirio Diaz, obtained concessions for the railroad and the colony. He then chartered a corporation, Credit Foncier, in New Jersey.

People buying stock in Credit Foncier received the right to join the colony, which was to be run communally and without the use of money. Work was to be assigned according to each person's ability, with credits awarded for labor. Individual accumulation of wealth was prohibited. Eight hours of work, eight hours of sleep and eight hours of culture or entertainment were to make up the daily routine. Colonists would build, own, and operate the railroad, telegraphs, banks, and water supply. Capital gained would be reinvested in the colony's infrastructure.

Credit Foncier clubs sprang up in the United States and Europe. In late 1886 the first 27 colonists arrived from California, and within a short time the population grew to 2,000.

Activities were directed by Owen. A team made daily trips to the Rio Fuerte to gather fresh water. Several towns were founded, connected by paved roads which permitted bicycle travel. Irrigation ditches were dug. A school was opened. Community theater grew, and an Academy of Sciences, with ties to the Smithsonian Institute, was founded.

Governed by the principles of order, industry and courtesy, the colonists attained modest economic success from fishing, farming and hunting. But the colony was growing much faster than Owen had envisioned. It became top heavy—too many planners and not enough workers.

Benjamin Johnson, only 25 years old when he arrived at the colony, challenged Owen's leadership and focused the colonies efforts toward developing a single cash crop—sugar. He received a concession to build a canal from the Rio Fuerte to what became Los Mochis, then convinced the Mexican government to evict most of the Owen colonists.

Owen left, but continued to work on building the railroad, convincing Arthur E. Stilwell, an American railroad owner, to join with him. In 1900 the Kansas City, Mexico and Orient Railroad, precursor to the Chihuahua al Pacifico line, was chartered. The same year the colony was abandoned, having lasted fourteen years.

Today, travelers flying into Los Mochis to begin their tour of Copper Canyon look down on the huge bay and the endless agricultural land, laid out in neat rectangular plots. Little remains of the Owen Utopia, but the area's rich farmlands, and the Copper Canyon railroad are the results of his vision.

The Central Plaza in El Fuerte is a place to sit on a bench and watch the local people go about their business. El Fuerte, "The Fort," was founded in 1564 as a frontier outpost and trading center.

El Fuerte

In 1610, the Viceroy of Montesclaros, viceroy of Mexico and Peru, ordered that a riverside fort be erected on a hill overlooking the town of San Juan Bautista de Carapoa, to defend it against attacks by fierce Mayo, Zuaque and Tehueco Indians, and to guard the rich haul of silver from its many mines. Founded fifty years earlier by the Spanish conquistador Don Francisco de Ibarra, the town was renamed El Fuerte, "The Fort."

In successive years, El Fuerte became a major trading post for gold and silver from the mines of Urique, Batopilas, and other Sierra Madre settlements and a station on Spain's fabled Camino Real trade route. In 1824, after almost three centuries as the most important commercial and agricultural center in northern Mexico, El Fuerte became the capital of the territory which now makes up the Mexican states of Sinaloa and Sonora, and part of Arizona. After a few years, and a few wars, its administrative functions were taken over by Culiacán, Hermosillo and Phoenix.

El Fuerte today, with a population of around 30,000, is a quiet, picturesque colonial town, but the old fort still looks down on the quaint cobblestone streets as they wind past its historic church, mansions and shops, many dating back to colonial times.

Most of El Fuerte's historic houses are set off the cobblestone streets leading from the central plaza. A number of them have been converted into government offices. The Hotel Villa Del Pescador, was built as a colonial home in the late 1800's. The Hotel Posada Hidalgo was built in 1890 by Señor Rafael Almada, a wealthy and influential *alcalde* (mayor), who spent five years and 100,000 gold pesos in its construction. The wooden trim was made from 285 Canadian wooden beams, which like much of the lavish furniture, were brought by boat from San Francisco, California, and unloaded at Topolobompo Bay at the time that Albert K. Owen's "colonia" was flourishing. The Cultural Center, *Casa de la Cultura*, was originally known as the "House of Vaults." It was built in the 18th century by Don Esteban Nicolas de la Vega y Colon from Portugal. More recently, up until 1979, the building was used as the city jail.

Arthur Edward Stilwell, a 19th century American visionary and railroad owner, along with Albert Kimsey Owen, was responsible for the building of Mexico's spectacular Copper Canyon Railroad.

Working on the Railroad

By Don Fuchik

The Chihuahua al Pacifico Copper Canyon rail journey through the Sierra Tarahumara is one of the world's most dramatic train rides. Spectacular in scenery and engineering, the line spans 37 bridges, passes through 86 tunnels and rises 8,000 feet in the 410 mile trip from Los Mochis to Chihuahua City.

This amazing rail line owes its creation to the farsightedness and creativity of two 19th century American visionaries—Albert Kimsey Owen and Arthur Edward Stilwell.

A Pennsylvania-born civil engineer, Owen saw the enormous potential of the huge natural harbor at Topolobampo and conceived the idea of a Pacific to Atlantic rail route through Mexico's rugged Sierra Madre as a land bridge connecting markets in the Far East with Europe. He had worked as a surveyor on the Laredo-Mexico City Railroad and knew that another line could be built through the seemingly impenetrable Sierra. At this time the

French had failed in their attempt to build a waterway across Panama so a binational railroad seemed a more viable alternative.

But Owen was a dreamer and turned his efforts to founding a utopian American colony at Topolobampo. The colony failed after only five years.

Another man, who had practical business skills as well as vision, carried on the quest for the railroad. He was Arthur Edward Stilwell, scion of a wealthy Rochester, New York family, who, at age 32, became the nation's youngest railroad owner.

Stilwell planned his rail line to run from Kansas City to Presidio, Texas, then join a Mexican line across the Rio Grande at Ojinaga, which would run through the state of Chihuahua and cross the Sierras to reach Topolobampo—several hundred miles shorter than the Union Pacific's Kansas City to San Francisco line.

Financing was obtained in the U.S. from local communities and oil companies, and in Mexico by the government of Porfirio Diaz promising land and cash concessions to wealthy entrepreneurs including Enrique Creel and Luis Terrazas.

Construction began and the tracks pushed forward throughout the 1890's. The Topolobampo-El Fuerte segment was completed in 1903, followed by the Chihuahua-Creel section in 1907.

Then the Mexican Revolution began in 1910 and over the next ten years put a stop to the project—the Mexican government could not meet its economic commitments, and Pancho Villa attacked the trains. Villa was miffed at being snubbed by Luis Terrazas at a ceremony celebrating the completion of a portion of the route. Terrazas correctly believed that Villa had been rustling his cattle. Because of all this, the Stilwell interests were forced into receivership.

Plans to complete the railroad languished for the next twenty years. Then, in 1940, President Lazaro Cardenas nationalized Mexico's railroads and announced that the government would complete the several hundred kilometers that still remained to be built. In 1941 the remaining route was surveyed and, on November 22, 1961, the first train arrived in Los Mochis from Chihuahua—almost a century after Owen first had his vision.

The railroad was completed by the Mexican government at a cost of over a billion pesos, without foreign aid. A colossal project far beyond the capacities of most developing nations. Engineering marvels abound: the El Descanso Tunnel extends over 6,000 feet; the Chinipas Bridge is 355 feet high; the Rio Fuerte Bridge is over 1,600 feet long. The gentle curvature of the rails, the gradual grades never exceeding 2.5%, and widespread use of 6-mile long spans of rail make for a smooth and comfortable passage.

Railroad Log: El Fuerte to Creel

By Charles Rau

The Chihuahua al Pacfico Railroad was completed in November of 1961 and took 90 years and over 90 million dollars to complete. It is considered to be one of the major railroad engineering achievements in the world. Starting at near sea level at the Port of Topolobampo, the rail line climbs into the northwestern Sierra Madre and reaches an elevation of 8,071 feet near the Continental divide. The passenger line ends at Chihuahua City, some 300 miles from Los Mochis, Sinaloa. Along the route there are 86 tunnels and 37 bridges. One tunnel is over one mile in length, and while going through another tunnel at Temoris, the train makes a 180 degree turn. The railway courses its way through some of the most rugged and scenic parts of northwest Mexico and passes through four distinct biotic communities.

Kilometer posts can be seen on the left side of the train near the tracks. (1 km= .62 miles) The tunnels are numbered on the upper right hand side of the entrance along with the tunnel length in meters (1 meter = 3.3 feet)

Km 838, El Fuerte Station (elevation: 620 ft.)

The town of El Fuerte (about five miles from the station) was established in the 1500's on the El Camino Real as a military and agricultural center. From here you soon start to travel into the Sinaloa Thorn Forest biotic community.

Km 822

The Heriberto Cement plant is on the left.

Km 807, La Laguna

On the left in the distance is the reservoir behind the Miguel Hidalgo Dam. This dam on the Fuerte river stores water for irrigation for the agricultural area around Los Mochis and the Fuerte valley. It also produces hydro-electric power for the area.

Km 790, Loreto, (elevation: 1,130 ft.)

The train makes a short stop at this small town before proceeding to the Rio Fuerte bridge. From here it is about 10 minutes to the longest bridge over the Fuerte River.

Km 781, Rio Fuerte Bridge

This is the longest bridge on the route (1,657 ft.) It crosses the Rio Fuerte, the 11th longest river in Mexico. The river is the major source of water for the Fuerte valley. This is an excellent photographic spot, with the best vantage spots on the left side of the train. Take pictures from the open areas between the cars.

Km 753, El Descanso Tunnel, ("The Resting Place")

This is the first tunnel (coming from Los Mochis) on the route and also the longest (5,966 ft.).

Km 748, Rio Chinipas Bridge

This bridge crossing the Chinipas river is the tallest on the rail line, 350 ft. above the water. On the right side of the train you can see the beginning of the Colossio reservoir behind the recently completed Luis Donaldo Colossio Dam. This river separates the States of Sinaloa and Chihuahua.

Kms 720–709

This section offers some of the most scenic and exciting parts of the rail line. The train passes through about 16 tunnels while traveling above the Rio Septentrion. Here you can see the best examples of Sinaloan Thorn Forest. If you look near the river's edge you can see stands of Otate Cane Bamboo growing. Rock Figs and Sabal Palms are growing on the sheer rock cliffs along with Octopus Agave. If you keep an eye on the river below, on the right side of the train, you might be lucky enough to see a rare river otter. Sometimes small flocks of brilliant green parrots and military macaws can be seen. At the right time of the year, colorful wildflowers are abundant.

Km 707.1, Santa Barbara Bridge

The train makes its way along this curved bridge above the Rio Mina Plata before coming to the Temoris Station. Just before coming into the station look up from the right side of the train to see Bridal Veil Falls in a cleft on the cliff face.

Km 707, Temoris Station (elevation: 3,400 ft.)
The small town of Temoris is located at the top of the cliffs. This spot is where the two ends of the railroad were joined and where the rail-line was dedicated in November of 1961. Notice the large commemorative sign made from steel rail tracks. From Temoris the train snakes it's way from near the river to near the top of a ridge using three levels of tracks. In one tunnel (*La Pera* or "The Pear") the train makes a 180 degree turn while in the tunnel. In another 30 minutes you move from the Thorn Forests into Madrean Evergreen Woodland. It is possible to see Sabal palms and large bromeliads intermixed with oaks, pines and junipers.

Km 668, Bahuichivo, (elevation: 5,330 ft.)
Bahuichivo is a small lumbering town. 17 km from Bahuichivo is the small village of Cerocahui. From Cerocahui a mountain road leads to the bottom of one of the largest Barrancas (Urique) to the little village of Urique.

Km 662, Cuiteco
A Jesuit mission was founded here by Father Salvatierra in 1684 as a center for the local Tarahumara. Tarahumara ranchos start to become evident on the hillsides.

Km 636, San Rafael
The train makes a short stop here (15 Mexican minutes) to take on water and change crews. Some Tarahumara women usually are present to sell some of their unique baskets.

Km 626, Mansion Tarahumara
This castle-like structure on the right is one of the hotels in this area.

Km 624, Posada Barrancas Station
(elevation: 7,000 ft.) The train makes a short stop here before going on to Divisadero.

Km 622, Divisadero, (elevation: 7,200 ft.)
At this stop is a breathtaking overlook of the Copper Canyon. Here three major Barrancas come together. The Urique river is over 4,000 feet below the rim. The train stops here for 15 minutes.

Km 592, El Lazo ("The Loop")
At this point the train crosses over the tracks and over a tunnel it had just previously traveled on and through.

Km 583, Los Ojitos, (elevation; 8,071 ft.)
This is the highest point on the route. From here to Creel the train passes through Madrean Conifer Forest with spectacular vistas.

Km 572.5, Continental Divide
The train passes the Continental Divide.

Km 564, Creel, (elevation: 7,770 ft.)
The town was named after Enrique Creel, a former governor of the State of Chihuahua, who established the town as a center for the Tarahumara. Today Creel is a major lumbering town and tourism center.

Father Juan Maria de Salvatierra, *an Italian Jesuit, founded the mission church at Cerocahui in the year 1680. Today the little town is considered to be the most beautiful mountain village in southwestern Chihuahua.*

The Village of Cerocahui

Nestled in a picturesque valley surrounded by Mexico's magnificent Sierra Madre Mountains, is the little village of Cerocahui, the most beautiful of all the mountain villages of southwestern Chihuahua State.

Cerocahui, with its old mission church, was founded in 1680 by the Italian Jesuit, Juan Maria de Salvatierra. It is said that Father Salvatierra, who founded many missions in the area, considered this to be his favorite.

Over the centuries, the 300-year-old church, with its lovely stained glass windows, fell into disrepair. In 1948 it was extensively reconstructed. Services are now held there for the towns people and the local Tarahumara Indians, and the church also operates an Indian orphanage and boarding school.

Walking around Cerocahui, which has a population of around 600, you can find people with skills which seem to belong to a bygone era. There are cowboys, prospectors, blacksmiths, and a man who makes rawhide lariats.

Just a mile from "downtown" Cerocahui is the Paraiso del Oso Lodge, located in a picturesque valley, surrounded by large rock formations. The lodge is owned and operated by American Doug Rhodes, who takes pride in the delicious Mexican food served at his lodge and in the fine horses he offers to guests who wish to ride.

From the Lodge, you can travel to the bottom of the canyon and the old silver mining town of Urique. Established in 1612, Urique was active eight years before the first pilgrims landed on Plymouth Rock.

Doug and Ana Maria Rhodes, and grandson, with "Yogi Bear" formation in background.

The Bear's Paradise

By Lori Klein

As we saunter up to the door of the Paraiso del Oso Lodge, we are greeted by three dogs, a cat, and a large white goose known as "Pancho." The lodge is located in a secluded valley in Mexico's Sierra Madre mountains, surrounded by large, volcanically formed spires, one of which resembles Yogi Bear wearing his hat—hence the name *Paraiso del Oso*, Spanish for "Bear's Paradise".

We are met by Doug Rhodes, a smiling cowboy who boldly exclaims, "I'm glad y'all made it. Welcome to the Paraiso Del Oso."

Doug is the owner and founder of the lodge, located halfway between the town of Bahuichivo and the farming village of Cerocahui. Established in 1679, Cerocahui now has around 600 inhabitants, mostly Tarahumara Indians and *mestizos*.

Doug, or "Diego" as he is referred to in Mexico, was once a tour guide in Copper Canyon. As he tells it, he became so frustrated by the region's lack of reliable hotels, that he searched until he found a remote spot ideal for exploring the area's rich flora, fauna, and natural history. Here he built his lodge and ranch.

Born in a rural Ohio farming community, Doug has followed many diverse paths. He was an army sergeant, a NASA electrical technician, an editor, a deputy sheriff, a bodyguard, and now an inn keeper. His greatest passion is horses—he owns at least a dozen, and he brags that they are the best trained and equipped in Northern Mexico.

Diego is married to Ana Maria Chavez Gutierrez, a native Cerocahuian, whose family has a long and rich history in the area. Her grandfather was a famous miner who fought alongside Pancho Villa in the Mexican Revolution.

Diego and Ana contribute much to the area, furnishing outreach services to local Tarahumara families, and other community services including an annual Christmas party for local children.

At the Paraiso, guests can hike, ride horses, bike, explore historical towns, go birding, or just settle down with a good book in front of the large fireplace, sip a margarita, and relax.

A young Tarahumara girl carries her baby sister on her back. The Tarahumara are the least assimilated of all the tribes in North America. They practice subsistence farming in the remote canyons of Mexico's Sierra Madre.

Who are the Tarahumara?

By Lee Klein

In the summer of 1993 two of our California Native guides, Doug Stewart and Lynn Reineke, escorted a small group of Indians from the depths of Mexico's Copper Canyon to Leadville, Colorado, where they astounded the world of marathon racing by coming in first, second and fourth place in a 100 mile ultra-marathon race, wearing their native garb and sandals made out of discarded tires.

Who were these strangely-dressed people, who came from obscurity to outpace hundreds of experienced runners?

They call themselves the *Rarámuri*, the Runners, and they inhabit the rugged and remote area of mountains and canyons in Mexico known as the *Barrancas del Cobre* or Copper Canyon. They are known to the outside world as the Tarahumara.

No one knows how long the Tarahumara have lived in their rugged homeland. Archaeologists have found artifacts of people living in the area 3000 years ago, but it is not known if they were the ancestors of the present day Indians.

There is no recorded history of the Tarahumara prior to the coming of the Spaniards in the 16th century. Their first European contact may have been with Coronado's expedition as it passed through the Sierra Madres searching for the legendary Seven Golden Cities of Cibola. In 1607 the Jesuit missionary Father Juan Fonte established the first Jesuit mission in their territory.

During the next 150 years, the Jesuits built twenty-nine missions and introduced the Indians to Catholicism, domestic animals, the plow and the axe. Their influence came to an abrupt halt in 1767 when the King of Spain expelled their order from the New World. The Franciscans took over from the Jesuits, but their influence on the Tarahumara was minimal and the Indians were pretty much left alone until the Jesuits returned in 1900.

The Tarahumara have traditionally lived in isolated family units and small settlements. The Spaniards tried to bring them into more concentrated communities but the strong-willed Tarahumara managed to resist these efforts, and today a large number still live in small, isolated groups. During the time of the Jesuits, mineral wealth was discovered in the region and many Indians were forced to work as slaves in the mines. This and the encroachment of the Spaniards upon their lands, led to many bloody revolts throughout the 17th century.

Today the Tarahumara number around 50,000. They still inhabit the same region they have for centuries— the rugged Sierra Madre Occidental of northern Mexico. They live in caves and small wood or stone cabins and practice subsistence farming. The majority practice a form of Catholicism liberally intermixed with their traditional beliefs and ceremonies.

Among the peoples of North America, the Tarahumara are considered to be the most primitive, the least touched by modern civilization. They are also the most unmixed of any of the Indian tribes of Mexico.

Many of the men and most of the women still dress in their traditional styles. The ladies wear wide multiple skirts, full sleeved blouses, a head band or bandana, and a shawl for carrying a child or other objects on their backs. The little girls dress the same as their mothers and often carry a little brother or sister on their backs. The men wear a breechcloth held together by a wool girdle wrapped around the waist, a cloth head band, and a loose cotton shirt.

Running up and down the steep canyons is an important part of the Tarahumara culture, not only as a means of transportation and communication in this rugged area, but as a sport in which villages compete against each other. From the time they are small children the Tarahumara take great pride in their running skills.

In the Rarámuri philosophy, respect for others is of prime importance. They give greater value to persons than to objects, and business matters take second place to respect for human beings.

Of all the religious ceremonies of the year, Semana Santa, Easter, is the most important of the year. Their faces and bodies covered with white paint, a group of Tarahumaras celebrate Easter in their own unique way.

Easter in Copper Canyon

By Lee Klein

Easter in Copper Canyon is the most colorful time of year. Small towns which are sleepy most of the year now are full of tourists—both Mexican and foreign—who have come to see the Easter celebrations of the Tarahumara Indians. The tourists cluster with their cameras in the Indian villages, but most of them have little idea of what is going on.

To begin to understand the Tarahumara ceremonies, one has to have a basic understanding of the Indians' religion. The Tarahumaras are outwardly Catholic, but their version of Catholicism is unlike any form we are familiar with.

In 1602, the Jesuits brought Christianity to the Indians, who adopted it, but interpreted and modified it to conform to their own customs and ideas. In 1767, King Charles III of Spain expelled the Jesuits from the New World, and the Tarahumaras, on their own now, continued to develop their religious beliefs and rituals. Their resulting theology is as follows:

God is the father of the Tarahumara and is associated with the sun. His wife, the Virgin Mary, is their mother and is associated with the moon. God has an elder brother, the Devil, who is the uncle of the Indians. The Devil is the father of all non-Indians, whom the Tarahumara call *chabóchi*, "whiskered ones". At death, the souls of the Tarahumara ascend to heaven while those of the *chabóchi* go to the bottommost level of the universe.

The well-being of the Tarahumara depends on their ability to maintain the proper relations with God and the Devil. God is benevolent, but they must not fail to reward His attentions adequately. The Devil is the opposite, and will cause the Indians illness and misfortune unless they propitiate him with food. God is pleased by the dancing, chanting, feasting, and offerings of food and corn beer, that are a part of all Tarahumara religious festivals. The Devil is also pleased because the Indians bury food for him at these fiestas.

Of all the religious ceremonies throughout the year, Easter is the most important. Hundreds of men, women, and children converge on the local church from villages as far away as fifteen miles. These celebrations are for socializing and having a good time, but the Indians also expect their efforts to please God so that He will give them long lives, abundant crops, and healthy children.

The Easter rituals concern the relationship between God and the Devil. Although God and the Devil are brothers, and occasionally get along, the Devil is usually bent on destroying God. Most of the time God fends the Devil off. But each year, immediately prior to Holy Week, the Devil succeeds by trick or force in rendering God dangerously vulnerable. The Easter ceremonies are intended to protect and strengthen God so that He can prevent the Devil from destroying the world.

Each of the men and boys of the community takes part in the ceremonies as a member of one of two groups. The first group, the Pharisees, are the Devil's allies, and carry wooden swords, painted white with ocher designs. The second group, the *Soldados*, the Soldiers, are allied with God, and carry bows and arrows.

The celebrations begin on the Saturday prior to Palm Sunday, with speeches and ritualized dances. The Pharisees, their bodies smeared with white earth, and the *Soldados*, dance to the beating of drums and the melody of reed whistles. About midnight, a mass is held in the church. Shortly after sunrise, bowls of beef stew, stacks of tortillas and tamales and bundles of ground, parched maize, are lifted to the cardinal directions, allowing the aroma to waft heavenward to be consumed by God. The food is then distributed among the people. At mid-morning the *Soldados* and Pharisees set up wooden crosses marking the stations of the cross, a mass is held, and the priest leads a procession around the churchyard, with the participants carrying palm branches.

Three days later, on Holy Wednesday, the ceremonies resume, and for the next three days there are processions around the church. The point of the processions is to protect the church and, by extension, God and God's wife.

On the afternoon of Good Friday, the Pharisees appear with three figures made of wood and long grasses representing Judas, Judas's wife, and their dog. To the Indians, Judas is one of the Devil's relatives, and they call him Grandfather and his wife Grandmother. Judas and his wife wear Mexican-style clothing and display their oversized genitalia prominently. The Pharisees and *Soldados* parade the figures around the church, dancing before them. The Pharisees then hide the figures away for the night.

On Saturday morning, the *Soldados* and Pharisees engage in wrestling matches, battling symbolically for control of Judas. The *Soldados* then take possession, shoot arrows into the three figures and set them afire. The people then retire to continue the celebrations at the many *tesguino* drinking parties held in the surrounding countryside.

Despite the glum predictions of their imminent extinction, by 19th Century anthropologist Carl Lumholz, the Tarahumara Indians still inhabit the caves and simple homesteads in Copper Canyon and continue to be the most populous indigenous group of northern Mexico.

Surviving and Thriving

By Don Fuchik

Anthropologist Carl Lumholtz predicted that the Tarahumara Indians would disappear within a century. A hundred years later, these gentle people, who inhabit Mexico's Copper Canyon, continue to be the most populous indigenous group in northern Mexico.

Spanish explorers had entered the Sierra Madre Mountains by the mid-16th century. Gold and silver were soon discovered and mines began operating. The Indians were pressed into the labor force, often enduring the harshest conditions.

The Jesuits established their first mission pueblo in 1611. Although many attempted to ease the burden of the Indians, a great deal of prejudice existed. An early Jesuit wrote, "They are inclined to idleness, drunkenness and other vices. They are ungrateful, dull and stupid...very cunning and alert in evil things...They have no sense of personal honor nor the honor of their daughters."

Forced to live in artificially-created communities, the Indians were susceptible to a variety of diseases, and epidemics swept the area. As the demand for labor increased, the Spanish raided the mission pueblos. The Jesuits managed to protect some of their charges, but many Tarahumara fled, hiding deep in Copper Canyon. The expulsion of the Jesuits from the Americas, in 1767, ended their efforts to protect the Indians, and the Franciscans, who succeeded them, were not as effective.

Mexico attained independence in 1821 and soon established huge land grants in Tarahumara country. The Indians were uprooted again, and fled, often onto lands of other indigenous people. Fighting often resulted.

The Revolution of 1910-21 resulted in the recreation of the pre-hispanic communal landholding system known as the *ejido*. The Tarahumara received some benefits from this, as much of this land has economic potential for lumbering, agriculture, and tourism. Around 50,000 Tarahumara still inhabit caves and simple dwellings in Copper Canyon.

The California Native has for many years assisted these people, donating clothing, school supplies and money. Some of our travelers have returned to volunteer in local clinics. Tourism is a positive factor, and visitors gain a new appreciation for these noble people who have survived and thrived despite Lumholtz' dire predictions.

Patracinio, a Tarahumara craftsman, produces handmade violins in Copper Canyon. The violin was introduced to the Tarahumara by the Spaniards during the 15th century.

The Best Violin Maker

Patracinio is a successful man. He owns two houses—a winter house located in the bottom of the canyon, only a two-and-a-half hour hike from the town of Batopilas, and a summer house at the top, a six-hour hike from the village of Samachique. He has a pretty wife, three kids, three burros, 30 to 40 goats and a few sheep. He also has the reputation of being the best violin maker in Copper Canyon.

Both of his houses are typically Tarahumara. They are made up of a combination of loosely fashioned together materials, mostly hand-hewn timbers, adobe, and piled up stones, with a wood shake roof. They have one room for eating and sleeping and one storage room. Outside the house are a corn crib and a work shed where Patracinio crafts his violins. Furnishings are simple; the family sleeps on straw mats and cooking is done over an open fire.

Like most Tarahumara, Patricinio is a subsistence farmer. He feeds his family by growing corn, beans and squash. During the slow season he has time to devote to his true love—making his violins. He sells the violins to other Tarahumara, who highly prize them, and to the Mission Store in Creel, where they are resold to the tourists. The sales provide him with cash to purchase the store-bought items that the family needs, such as coffee, lard, salt, sugar, matches and cotton cloth.

Patricinio's wife, Aurelia, is a homemaker. She cooks the meals, washes the clothes, cleans the house and tends the children. She also makes and sells baskets to supplement the family income.

His three daughters, Marca, Felicia, and Paola, ages 5, 4, and 2, also have their jobs. Six times a day they hike the 500 yards to the gorge with buckets on their heads to fetch water from the stream; often the 2-year-old is carried in a shawl on her older sisters back.

The girls are also responsible for keeping the goats out of the cornfields. They are experts at throwing rocks which land alongside any goat who gets too close.

The goats are very important to the feeding of the family—but not as a source of meat. At night they are kept in a small portable log corral. The corral is set up over a dormant field and every few days is taken apart and moved along the rows. In this way the fields are fertilized and are ready to be planted for next year's crop.

Around 1300 miles northwest of Patracinio's home is the home of California Native guide Doug Stewart. Doug is a friend of Patracinio's.

The two men met during the Kórima food program which Doug and his partner, California Native guide Lynn Reinecke, instituted in the winter of 1983 to help the Indians survive the previous year's crop failure. Since both Doug and Patracinio are craftsmen—Doug specializing in woodworking and ceramics—they became good friends. Doug now visits Patracinio and his family several times a year.

When Doug first met Patricinio, Patracinio's violin making tools consisted of three cheap Mexican pocket knives, a hacksaw blade with a rag wrapped around it, an awl made from an old nail, an old spike filed into a chisel, broken glass used for scraping, a bent knife made from a car spring, and rope and pieces of wood for clamps. With these makeshift tools Patracinio produced six violins a year.

After his first visit, Doug consulted with American violin makers and studied the techniques and tools needed to produce hand crafted violins. On his subsequent visits Doug brought Patracinio gifts of quality violin making tools: high carbon steel knives, chisels, gouges, saws, awls, twist drills and planes; violin clamps, a diamond sharpening stone, sand paper and varathane varnish.

With the new tools, the quality of Patracinio's violins as well as the quantity he can produce have greatly improved. He now makes twice as many in a year and the extra revenue benefits his family.

Patracinio has given Doug some of his finest violins—a gift, which to Doug, cannot be valued in terms of money—a gift of friendship and mutual appreciation between two people of widely different cultures.

Considered by many to be the world's greatest long distance runners, the Tarahumaras run for sport up and down the magnificent canyons of Mexico's Sierra Madres.

Tarahumaras Run to Win

In August of 1993, California Native guides Doug Stewart and Lynn Reinecke escorted a team of seven Tarahumara Indians from Mexico's Copper Canyon to Leadville, Colorado, where they competed against 294 runners from around the world in the Leadville Trail 100, a one hundred mile ultra-marathon race.

The annual race begins and ends at Leadville, in the heart of the Rocky Mountains, and follows a punishing mountain course which winds through the Sawatch Range, twice rising to an altitude of 12,600 feet. The runners were further handicapped by cold rain.

Competing against highly trained runners, the Tarahumaras, with no special training, ran in sandals made from discarded tires, which Lynn and Doug salvaged from the Leadville dump. Instead of running shorts they wore their traditional costumes.

Victoriana Churro, a 55-year-old Tarahumara, won the race with a 40 minute lead. Tarahumaras Cerrildo Chacarito, 38, and Manuel Luna, 30, placed second and fifth. Churro's winning time was 20 hours, two minutes and 33 seconds.

This was the first time these people had left their native state of Chihuahua and, during the trip, they discovered a new favorite food: pizza. During the race, they kept up their energy with a more traditional Tarahumara food, *piñole*, ground cornmeal mixed with water.

The cave-dwelling Tarahumara people grow up running on the steep mountain trails amidst the spectacular scenery of Copper Canyon.

A Tarahumara farm lies deep in one of the beautiful canyons which make up the complex of mountains and canyons known as Copper Canyon.

The Visit

By Doug Stewart

The morning was clear and sunny in Samachiqui Canyon, deep in Mexico's Sierra Madre mountains, a relief after the fierce storm of the previous night. As I sat outside of my tent, I watched the old Tarahumara man make his way down a side canyon and head towards my camp. He walked very slowly with the aid of a stick. I could not guess how old he really was, but the years of sun and weather had etched a grand network of deep lines into his face.

As he came closer I greeted him with the Tarahumara equivalent of "Hello." We shook hands in the Tarahumara method—lightly brushing our hands past one another. He told me his name was Wawalupi.

I made a remark about the rain last night, and he nodded his head in affirmation. We visited together, conversing with gestures, smiles, Spanish, and a little of the Tarahumara language. Our conversation was accompanied by long periods of silence, as is customary with the Tarahumara people.

His visit was not unexpected. Earlier that morning I had stumbled on his small house while I was exploring up a small canyon close to where I was camped. I had sat on a rock for over 30 minutes and waited for an invitation because it is the polite Tarahumara thing to do. Though the occupants knew of my presence, no contact was made at that time, not unusual for the shy Tarahumara.

As we visited, I gave the old man a cup of their traditional *pinole* (toasted ground corn usually mixed with water).

"*Muy rico,*" he commented.

"Yes, very tasty," I agreed in Spanish.

As he left my camp, he peered into the back of my pickup's camper shell, and stopped dead in his tracks. It was not something foreign that caused his reaction, but the fact that the whole back of my truck was filled with bags of corn and beans—so much food during a time of very bad drought.

"What is that?" he asked.

"Food, beans and corn," I replied.

"Who is it for?" he wanted to know.

I told him I was waiting for the Tarahumara runners who live far down in the canyons. Part of the food was for their families so that they could go to the United States to run. The rest was to trade with them for crafts. He thought about this for a long time, said good-bye, and left.

A few hours later he returned carrying a bag from which he slowly brought out an old woven wool sash.

"Will you trade some food for this *faja?*" he asked.

It was a nice old belt and I had lots of food, so I agreed. As he left, I could see he was pleased with the transaction.

Later that afternoon, he returned with his wife who way carrying a large old basket. "She would like to trade the basket for some food," he informed me. Knowing that they were short of food made it hard to decide how much corn to offer.

The next morning he brought his mother, who looked as old as the canyon rocks. On her back she carried a huge bundle wrapped in a blanket which she lowered to the ground in slow-motion. It contained a giant old clay pot used for making *tesgüino*, their traditional corn beer. She wanted to trade the pot for food. I made a rough estimate of what I hoped the pot was worth, plus a little fudge-factor, and came up with a fair sized pile of corn and beans. They both seemed very pleased. It took the two of them to carry off the food.

The old man returned again the following morning, this time not to trade but to present me with a giant yard-long carved wooden spoon, the spoon that went with the beer pot.

That afternoon, the runners I had been waiting for showed up, the food was distributed, and I took my leave. I was a little sad to leave the area, as I had enjoyed my time with the old man. Every time I look at the giant wooden spoon hanging on my wall I think back to my time in Samachique Canyon and remember Wawalupi, the old Tarahumara gentleman.

A young Tarahumara mother receives health care for her child at the Clinic of Santa Teresita. Founded by Father Luis Verplancken, a Jesuit priest, the clinic is funded primarily by donations and furnishes hospital care for thousands of Tarahumara children.

Clinic of Santa Teresita

Deep in the heart of Mexico's Sierra Madres, in the town of Creel, the center of Copper Canyon country, is the clinic of Santa Teresita. The lives of thousands of Tarahumara Indian children have been saved here because of the dreams and dedication of one man, Father Luis Verplancken.

Father Verplancken is a Jesuit priest who first visited the Tarahumaras in the late 1950's. He saw a great need for health care for these Indians who inhabit this remote area of mountains and canyons. At the time their children had an alarmingly high mortality rate.

Verplancken put his ideas into action by starting a traveling health care facility, housed in 4-wheel drive station wagon. He quickly discovered that a little help went a long way—one dollar's worth of penicillin, for example, could treat hundreds of children.

The word spread and by 1964, Verplancken and his volunteers received enough donations to establish a small hospital in an old railroad warehouse. The demand for medical care was so great that some Tarahumaras walked three days from their remote villages to reach the hospital.

A major obstacle that both the town and the hospital faced was the lack of a dependable water supply. With the help of more donations, a pipeline was built from the nearest fresh water source, which was four miles away over extremely harsh terrain. Three handcrafted pumping stations had to be constructed to lift the water 600 feet up to the level of the town. For the first time, Creel and the hospital had a dependable supply of fresh water.

In the mid-1970s, plans were drawn for a more modern hospital. With the help of his nephew, who was studying architecture at the time, Verplancken designed what today is known as the clinic of Santa Teresita. This clinic was literally "handmade." Along with a dedicated group of volunteers, Father Verplancken quarried the stone, crafted the brick and cut the trees.

The clinic opened in 1979, and houses a seventy-bed hospital with x-ray and laboratory facilities, a pharmacy, dental facilities and an outpatient clinic.

Today, it still depends on volunteers and donors. Over 90% of the services and medications are provided free of cost, and the remainder are provided to the local residents at a token fee.

Many participants on California Native Copper Canyon trips have visited the clinic and donated money, medicines and supplies. One woman, after returning from a recent trip, sent four sets of crutches that she purchased at a garage sale in the United States.

The son of a wealthy American consul, Enrique (Henry) Clay Creel, namesake of the town of Creel, served as governor of the State of Chihuahua, 1904–1911, and made a fortune as a politician, and entreprenuer.

Creel Builds an Empire

By Lee Klein

With a scream of brakes the locomotive rumbled into the station to discharge passengers at the town of Creel, high in Mexico's Sierra Madre mountains, the jumping off place for trips into the vast area of Copper Canyon.

Founded in 1906, the town was the creation of Enrique (Henry) Creel, governor of the State of Chihuahua. He planned to create a mixed colony of Tarahumara and Mexican families, each of which would be given 25 acres of land. When the Tarahumaras refused to participate, the plan failed but the city of Creel eventually grew to its present population of 5,000.

History paints Creel as a brilliant entrepreneur, politician, and dreamer, but some view him as an opportunistic scoundrel whose actions added to the poverty which resulted in the Mexican Revolution.

Born into wealth in Chihuahua City, on August 30, 1854, Enrique was the son of President Lincoln's United States Consul in Chihuahua, Rubén W. Creel, and his Mexican wife.

After a privileged childhood, Enrique married Angela Terrazas, his first cousin and the daughter of Luis Terrazas, one of the wealthiest landowners in Northern Mexico. Together they accumulated a fortune—millions of acres of land, textile mills, railroads, haciendas, and ranches.

When Porfirio Diaz forced his way into the presidency of Mexico, in 1876, the wealthy, elite landowners, including the Terrazas and Creels, gained even more wealth. Typical of his political machinations, Diaz appointed Creel a director of the National Company of Dynamite and Explosives. Mexico's demand for explosives was high because of its mining industry and its army's need for munitions. The board imposed an 80% import tax on dynamite, which allowed its members to manufacture explosives without competition.

In 1904, Creel became governor of Chihuahua. As governor, he enacted laws that permitted the sale of underutilized community land to outsiders, and many residents became landless laborers. Because of the resulting unemployment and the economic depression of 1907-08, Chihuahua became a center of revolutionary activity.

The revolution broke out in 1910, and three years later, Pancho Villa expropriated much of the Terrazas-Creel wealth. During these turbulent times, Creel moved to the United States. Twenty years later, he returned to Mexico, resumed his banking business and served as advisor to President Obregón. He died on August 18, 1931 at the age of seventy-seven.

During his lifetime he was involved in countless corporations and agencies that shaped the development of Mexico's economy and government, and served as a member of the Mexican National Congress, Ambassador to the U.S., Governor of Chihuahua, and Minister of Foreign Affairs. He founded scientific societies, banks, telephone companies and railroads, and played an important role in the construction of the Chihuahua al Pacifico Railroad—the scenic portal to Copper Canyon.

A cowboy leads his horses up a quiet street in the little town of Batopilas. All is quiet here now, but In the 19th century, Batopilas was one of the richest silver mining towns in the world.

Where Time Stands Still

By Lee Klein

A dusty cowboy rides his horse down the sunbaked-earth main street, his pistol at his side. A small group of Indians, clad in bright colored blouses, breech cloths and headbands, pack their burros for the long journey back to their remote village. Nearby a group of children play tag around the bougainvilleas in the town square.

This is Batopilas, a small village located in Mexico's Sierra Madres at the bottom of the deepest canyon in the vast complex of mountains and canyons known collectively as Copper Canyon. Today Batopilas is a sleepy little village, but it was not always this way. At the end of the 19th century it was one of the richest silver mining areas in the world.

The Spaniards first mined ore here in 1632, and the mines continued to produce for the next 300 years. In the late 1800's an American named Alexander Shepherd developed the mines to their highest level of production—ranking them among the richest silver mines in the world.

Today there is no large-scale mining in Batopilas, though a few old prospectors still pan gold and silver from the river or extract small quantities of ore from the abandoned workings.

Three miles downstream from Batopilas, past an old suspension bridge, is a 400-year-old Jesuit mission. The mission, recently restored, is known as the "Lost Cathedral" of Satevo, because over the course of time all records of it were lost by the Catholic Church.

Most of the buildings in Batopilas were built during the Victorian Era, though some date back to the 17th century. Many of the businesses have no signs on them—after all, in a town the size of Batopilas everyone knows where everything is. In the general store the counters are the old-fashioned high ones, worn smooth and wavy from a century of customers resting their elbows.

Evening is a special time in Batopilas. As the twilight spreads over the little town square the residents gather to visit with their neighbors, share the events of the day, and relax. Meanwhile, the youngsters play basketball until it is time for bed.

Traveling to Batopilas is an adventure in itself. Beginning in Creel, the road travels up and down through mountains and valleys and finally, just outside of the Tarahumara Indian village of Kirare, heads straight down along a windy, twisted, one-lane, dirt road to the bottom of the canyon. From there it hugs the side of the canyon as it follows the Rio Batopilas down river for another hour, finally arriving in Batopilas after 5½ to 8 hours, depending on whether you travel by car or take the local bus. The local bus is a rickety old school bus which makes the trip down from Creel every other day. For the return trip, the bus departs Batopilas at 4:30 a.m. so that it can reach the rim of the canyon before the radiator boils over.

The journey to Batopilas is a breathtaking trip, but is not suitable for all travelers as the road down may make the faint-of-heart wish they had stayed at home. The best time to make the journey down is in the winter time, because Summer temperatures can soar above 100° Fahrenheit.

To visit Batopilas is to take a trip back in time. When the Mexican War caused the mines to close, movement into the 20th century halted. The electric generators stopped turning, the Americans left, and the towns people returned to the slow traditional life of a rural Mexican village. The bustling mining boom town no longer existed.

Alexander Robey "Boss" Shepherd, last territorial governor of Washington D.C., developed the remote village of Batopilas, located in the bottom of Mexico's Copper Canyon, into one of the richest silver mining towns in the world.

Silver King of Batopilas

By Lee Klein

At the bottom of the deepest canyon in the vast complex of mountains and canyons known collectively as Copper Canyon is the sleepy little village of Batopilas. Sitting next to the bougainvilleas in the town square you might see a cowboy riding his horse down the sunbaked-earth main street, or a group of brightly clad Indians packing their burros for the long journey back to their remote village. It is hard to believe that this quiet village was once one of the richest silver mining cities in the world.

The Spaniards first mined ore here in 1632. Over the centuries more than three hundred mines were worked, but it took a most unusual American to bring real wealth to the area. The man was Alexander Shepherd and the story starts, not in this remote section of Mexico's Sierra Madre mountains, but in Washington D.C.

In 1871, Alexander Robey "Boss" Shepherd became territorial governor of the District of Columbia. At that time Washington was a city with muddy streets and unpaved sidewalks. During his three years in office Shepherd constructed 157 miles of roads, 123 miles of sewers, 39 miles of gas mains and 30 miles of water mains, leading some historians to refer to him as the "Father of Modern Washington." Instead of being heralded as a hero, however, he was ungraciously chased out of office after Congress discovered that he had overspent the cities budget by $16 million with a disproportionate share of the benefits going to neighborhoods in which he had financial interests.

Shepherd declared bankruptcy and, in 1880, moved his family to Batopilas, where he had purchased a silver mine from another American, John Robinson, for $600,000. Thirteen years earlier, Robinson bought two old supposedly worked out mines where he discovered a rich vein of ore, but then ran into a major obstacle—because of the remoteness of the area his transportation and processing costs were far too high to make the operation profitable.

Shepherd, who always thought on a grand scale, applied the same organizing skills he had used in Washington to his new mining venture.

He began by filing more than 300 additional mining claims and consolidating his holdings into the Batopilas Mining Company. Then, instead of shipping out raw ore to be processed at some distant location, he constructed a complete processing facility in Batopilas. The processed silver was cast into bars, loaded two bars per mule, and taken by monthly mule trains of up to 100 mules to Chihuahua.

Between 1880 and 1906, 20 million ounces of silver were extracted from the mines—ranking the Batopilas mines among the richest silver mines in the world. At their peak the mines employed 1500 workers, and the total length of tunnels exceeded 70 miles.

Shepherd's innovations included the construction of the Porfirio Diaz tunnel—a tunnel bored through the base of a mountain, where a train hauled out ore, which was dropped down shafts from the tunnels above. The train had to be dismantled and hauled in almost 200 miles by burro and human labor. The tunnel is still there, now deserted except by bats.

Shepherd did much to improve the town of Batopilas, building bridges, aqueducts, and a hydroelectric plant, which made Batopilas the second city in Mexico to have electricity—second only to Mexico City itself. By the time Shepherd died in 1902, the town's population had grown from 400 to around 5000 (it is now around 1000). The hydroelectric facility he built was restored in 1988 and once again powers the town, and his original aqueduct still provides the local water supply.

Spanish treasures of gold and silver may be buried in the vicinity of the church at Satevo, in the bottom of Batopilas Canyon. The church, is often referred to as the "Lost Cathedral" because its records were destroyed in a fire in the early 1800's.

The Treasure of the Sierra Madre

By Lee Klein

The beauty of Mexico's Copper Canyon and the simple lifestyle of its Tarahumara Indians is the real "Treasure of the Sierra Madre," but this remote region of rugged mountains and deep canyons may also hold more traditional treasure—gold and silver buried in undiscovered treasure troves.

In February, 1767, King Charles III of Spain decreed that all Jesuits be expelled from the New World and that their properties be confiscated. His counselors had advised him that the Jesuits held a special allegiance to the pope and opposed the supremacy of the monarchy. In addition, there were suspicions that the Jesuits were involved in political intrigues in Madrid. Some of this came about because the Jesuits, known as the "Black Robes," had acquired much wealth and power throughout the empire, causing enmity among clergy of other orders.

To prevent the Jesuits from hiding their wealth, it became imperative that the expulsion be carried out simultaneously and without warning throughout the empire. Messages under seal of the king were sent to all military commanders and were not to be opened until June 25. On that day the officers were ordered to arrest and deport the Jesuits and confiscate all the church's property for the crown.

Despite the best efforts at secrecy, the Jesuits in Mexico became aware of the plan and began conveying their treasure out of the country by secret channels. Because of the short notice, they could not transport all of the gold and silver and were forced to bury large quantities of it.

In the bottom of Copper Canyon, four miles beyond the town of Batopilas, is Satevo, a small settlement with a beautiful old church, *Iglesias San Miguel de Satevo*. The church, with its three-tiered bell tower and its three domes, is all that remains of the mission of *Santo Angel Custodio de Satevo*, built by the Jesuits around 1760 and destroyed by a fire in the late 1800's. All of the mission's records were lost in the fire and the church has become fancifully known as the "Lost Cathedral of Satevo."

In the 1800's, vandals looking for wealth hidden by the Jesuits, ransacked the church and its crypts, but there is no evidence that they found anything. Some people believe that treasure is still hidden in the vicinity of the old church and, indeed, throughout the Sierra Madre mountains.

On your journey to the bottom of the canyon you probably won't uncover the gold and silver allegedly buried by the Jesuits, but among the beauty, tranquility, and the always-present history of the region, you're sure to discover your own "Treasure of the Sierra Madre."

Over 50,000 Mennonites live in the state of Chihuahua near the city of Cuauhtémoc. Prior to the Mexican Revolution, the land which they now occupy was owned by newspaper magnate William Randolph Hearst.

The Mennonites

By Lee Klein

A man wearing a black wide-brimmed hat and a long black coat drives his horse-and-buggy to the market. He passes farms where blond-haired children work in the fields, the girls wearing large "Little-House-on-the-Prairie" bonnets and wide skirts, the boys wearing striped bib-overalls and straw hats. This scene, reminiscent of an earlier time in the United States, still takes place today in the Mexican state of Chihuahua.

In 1922, at the invitation of President Alvaro Obregón, 20,000 Mennonites came to Mexico from Canada to settle on 247,000 acres of land in Chihuahua's San Antonio Valley.

The immigration was profitable for both Mexico and the Mennonites. In Canada there had been friction between the Mennonites and the Canadian government—the Mennonites do not believe in educating their children past the sixth grade, else they become too worldly and stray from their religion, and they do not believe in serving in the military. The

Mexican government was seeking farmers to settle the land which had previously been owned by William Randolph Hearst, who had been expelled from the country along with the other foreign landowners, following the Mexican Revolution. The two parties made an agreement whereby the Mennonites would purchase the land from the Mexican government and their children would be forever exempted from the educational laws of Mexico and from serving in its armed forces. In addition, the Mennonites were exempted from paying taxes for fifty years.

Today, there are around 50,000 Mennonites living in the vicinity of the city of Cuauhtémoc, which is located about sixty-five miles west of the capital city of Chihuahua. They are known throughout Mexico for the fine cheeses they produce and for the wheat, corn, and oats which they grow.

The Mennonites trace their roots back to 16th century Europe. The Anabaptists, preachers of adult baptism, were persecuted for their beliefs, and many emigrated. The Mennonites take their name from Menno Simons, a 16th century Dutch Anabaptist leader, who laid down many of the principles of their faith. Perhaps the most important of these principles was that of forming spiritual communities in which the faithful would live apart from the secular world and remain close to the soil.

The Mennonites, along with the Mexican farmers, city-dwellers, and Tarahumara Indians, add to the wonderful cultural mix of northern Mexico.

The Chihuahua Cathedral took almost a century to complete. Dedicated to Saint Francis of Assisi, in 1727, It was completed in the 19th century with donations from Chihuahua's silver barons.

¡Ay Chihuahua!

By Don Fuchik

Copper Canyon travelers look forward to the wonders of the train ride into the Sierra Madre, visiting the quaint mining town of Batopilas at the bottom of the canyon, and meeting the elusive Tarahumara Indians, but few give much thought to the sights to be enjoyed at the end of the journey in Chihuahua City.

The *Quinta Luz* (Luz's Mansion), home of revolutionary hero Pancho Villa, was completed in 1909. Here Luz Corral, Villa's widow, lived and held court to thousands of visitors, until her death on June 6, 1981. She willed the residence to the government, which then restored it as a national museum, the *Museo de la Revolución Mexicana* (Museum of the Mexican Revolution). The fifty rooms that used to board Villa's bodyguards have been converted into exhibition rooms displaying artifacts of Chihuahua's cultural and revolutionary history. Among must-see items is the bullet riddled car Villa was driving when he was assassinated, at the age of 45, in 1923.

The *Quinta Gameros* (Gameros Mansion) houses a beautiful collection of noveau art furniture and hosts many art exhibits. It was built by Don Manuel Gameros, between 1907 and 1910, and, according to legend, was to be a wedding gift to his much younger bride, Rosa Terrazas. Rosa jilted him and the Revolution caused him to flee to the U.S., where he died before he could return to Chihuahua.

The *Palacio Del Gobierno* (The Palace of the Governor) offices the legislative, judicial and executive branches of the state government. Originally a Jesuit school for the sons of rich Spanish families, it was the site of the execution of Miguel Hidalgo, father of Mexico's independence. The interior courtyard has a panoramic mural, painted in 1960-62 by Aaron Piña Mora, depicting the history of the state of Chihuahua from the earliest arrival of the Spanish to the Revolution of 1910. Peña Mora included himself in the mural—he is the man with glasses in the eastern corner.

A short pedestrian mall connects the *Palacio* with the *Plaza de Armas*, with its statue of Antonio Daza y Ulloa, founder of the city. At the far end of the plaza is the magnificent cathedral, which took almost a century to complete. Dedicated to Saint Francis of Assisi, in 1727, the cathedral was completed with donations from the silver barons of the 19th century. Construction was stopped several times by the Apache and Comanche Indian wars. Both the facade and the spectacular main altar inside are of Italian marble.

Chihuahua City doesn't rank as a major tourist destination in Mexico, but it makes my short list of great Mexican cities.

Considered to be the father of his country, Miguel Hidalgo y Costilla, a Catholic priest, started the Mexican War of Independence which resulted in Mexico's becoming an independent country.

The Father of Mexico

By Lee Klein

He was a 57-year-old priest whose parish was in the city of Dolores, Guanajuato. The date was September 16, 1810. Early that morning Father Miguel Hidalgo y Costilla had the church bells rung to summon the towns-people to the church, where he told his followers that the time had come to expel the Spaniards who had misgoverned Mexico for so long. His speech, known as the *Grito de Dolores*, the "Cry of Dolores," set off the Mexican War of Independence, which resulted in Mexico's becoming an independent country.

Hidalgo was born in 1753 on the hacienda where his father was administrator. At twenty years of age he received his Bachelor of Theology degree and lectured in philosophy and theology at San Nicolás Obispo and, after being ordained as a priest, became rector of the school. His ideas and conduct were extremely liberal, which led to his being dismissed from that post, and twice being investigated by the Inquisition, who accused him of reading prohibited books, advocating doctrines of the French Revolution, doubting the virgin birth of Mary, gambling, and keeping a mistress. His last clerical position was that of parish priest in the little town of Dolores.

Hidalgo worked hard to improve the lives of his parishioners, mastering their Indian language and teaching them crafts and skills to improve their economic condition. He also introduced winemaking and silk culture, two industries which the government declared illegal in the colonies, and one day government officials came to the village and destroyed the vines and mulberry trees.

Late in the 18th century it became fashionable among cultured *criollos*, persons of Spanish descent who were born in Mexico, to form literary societies, which met for tea and cakes and discussed the classics. They also smuggled into the country books which were banned by the Church, such as the works of Rousseau, Voltaire, and Descartes. The literary societies gradually became political societies. Father Hidalgo belonged to one of these societies whose members were plotting a revolution to separate Mexico from Spain.

The group selected Hidalgo to lead the movement, and thus on the morning of September 16th, 1810, Hidalgo, with his "Cry of Dolores" launched the revolution, and the rebel army set forth, armed with machetes, swords, knives, clubs, axes, and a few muskets. As they passed through each town they opened the local jails and recruited the prisoners for their cause. Eventually their numbers grew to sixty thousand.

After six months of fighting, Hidalgo fell into a royalist trap and was captured. Because he was a priest, he was subjected to a lengthy hearing by the Inquisition, after which he was found guilty of heresy and treason, defrocked, and, on July 30, 1811, executed by a firing squad in the city of Chihuahua. His head, along with those of three other revolutionary leaders, was cut off and sent to Guanajuato, where it was put on a pole and displayed for a decade.

After Hidalgo's death, the revolutionary movement continued until September 28,1821, when Mexico finally became an independent nation.

In Mexico, Hidalgo is credited with arousing the spirit of rebellion against the Spanish oppression. Because of his patriotism, his championing of human rights and his personal courage, he is considered by Mexicans to be the father of their nation and the symbol of Mexican independence.

Each year on September 15, Independence Day is celebrated throughout Mexico, with parades, fireworks, and the cry of "Mexicanos, Viva Mexico!"

Francisco "Pancho" Villa, shown here in a portrait which hangs in Chihuahua's Museum of the Revolution, was considered by some to be a hero and Robin Hood, and by others to be a cold-blooded killer and villain.

Who Was Pancho Villa?

By Lee Klein

Pancho Villa, so the saying goes, was "hated by thousands and loved by millions." He was a Robin Hood to many and a cruel, cold-blooded killer to others. But who was this colorful controversial hero of the Mexican Revolution and where did he come from?

Doroteo Arango, for that was Pancho Villa's real name, was born in the state of Durango in 1878, a sharecropper peasant on a hacienda. According to the legend, one day when he was sixteen, he returned home from the fields to find that his sister had been raped by the owner of the hacienda, Don Agustin López Negrete. Doroteo took up his revolver, shot Don Agustin, and escaped into the mountains on a horse.

He became a cattle rustler and later joined a band of rustlers that was led by a man named Francisco "Pancho" Villa. In one of their many skirmishes with the law, the group was surprised by a group of *ruales* (mounted police) and Francisco was killed. Doroteo then took command of the gang and also assumed the name of the fallen leader. He may have done this to throw off those who hunted him for the murder of the hacienda owner or he may have done this to insure his authority over the group. Anyway, from that time on it was he who was known as Francisco "Pancho" Villa.

Pancho Villa was a natural leader and was very successful as a bandit, leading raids on towns, killing, and looting. He was also involved in more legitimate ventures, including being a contractor on the Copper Canyon railroad.

In 1910, when the Mexican Revolution broke out, Villa was recruited by the revolutionary leader, Abraham Gonzalez. Villa put together an army of armed cowboys and ruffians and became the revolutionary general who led the war in the northern part of Mexico. His charisma and victories made him an idol of the masses.

In 1916, when an American merchant refused to deliver the arms to Villa's army which they had paid him for, Villa entered the United States and raided the town of Columbus, New Mexico. He was pursued by General "Black Jack" Pershing through the mountains of the State of Chihuahua. Pershing's pursuit of Villa ended in failure, causing him to telegraph back to Washington that "Villa is everywhere, but Villa is nowhere."

The war ended in 1920, and many attempts were made on Villa's life by relatives of persons he had killed. On July 20, 1923, while driving his car through the town on Parral, Durango, he was assassinated. The men responsible were never identified.

California Native guide Don Fuchik (standing) and his father, Jim Fuchik, visit Luz Corral de Villa, widow of Pancho Villa, at her home in Chihuahua, Mexico, during 1974 trip through Mexico's Copper Canyon.

Visiting Mrs. Pancho Villa

By Don Fuchik

Sitting in her simple wooden chair, Doña Luz Corral de Villa, widow of Pancho Villa, began a rambling discourse on her life with the famous—or infamous—bandit, general, and hero of the Mexican Revolution.

The year was 1974, seven years before her death, when I first met Mrs. Villa. My father and I were touring Copper Canyon, and we were introduced to her at her home in the city of Chihuahua.

Sharing her memories with us, eighty-two-year-old Doña Luz told us of her life as a child, living with her widowed mother in the town of San Andres. One day, when she was a teenager, Villa and his soldiers rode in and demanded monetary contributions from the townspeople. Her mother asked to be excluded, and Villa visited her small store to see if she was really as poor as she claimed to be. There he met Luz. The courtship was very brief, and over the objections of her mother, Luz married Villa. The attending priest asked Villa to make his confession. The General refused, stating that it would take days to list all his sins.

Luz was not the only woman in Villa's life. He was linked with several in bogus marriages, but later Luz was able to produce a valid certificate proving that she was his only legal wife.

The couple had one child, a daughter, who died within a few years. Luz had no other children, but she took in children Villa had fathered with other women. Perhaps she felt that he would always return to her, knowing that several of his children were with her.

Villa built the quinta (manor) during the Revolution, and Luz lived there until her death in 1981. Villa was assassinated in 1923, and several of his "wives" claimed the manor. The marriage certificate might not have been sufficient to safeguard her claim, but Luz had an important ally, Alvaro Obregon, President of Mexico. During the Revolution, Obregon had visited the Villas at the quinta. There Villa had plotted to have Obregon killed, but Luz had interceded, saving the future president's life. The favor was not forgotten, and Obregon used his considerable influence to protect Luz's claim.

Eventually the house became a museum, with Luz the resident caretaker, and she tried personally to meet each visitor. Luz traveled through Mexico and the United States, and in Los Angeles received the key to the city.

Shortly before her death she wrote a book about her life with Villa, *Pancho Villa: an Intimacy*, published by Centro Librero La Prensa, in the city of Chihuahua. In it she loyally defends Villa against most of the accusations against him for his many excesses while leading the Army of the North. While this book must be read with a skeptical eye, her account provides interesting insights into Villa and the Revolution.

Archduke Maximilian, brother of Austria's Emperor Franz Joseph, was set up by Napoleon III as emperor of Mexico in 1864, after French troops took over the country. He was executed by a Mexican firing squad in 1867.

What is Cinco de Mayo?

In the United States we honor the Irish on Saint Patrick's Day, the Italians on Columbus Day, and the Mexicans on Cinco de Mayo. But what the heck is Cinco de Mayo?

Most Americans think that Cinco de Mayo (the 5th of May) celebrates Mexican Independence Day. Not so. Mexican Independence Day is September 16. Then what is Cinco de Mayo?

After Mexico won its independence from Spain in 1821, it went through forty years of internal power struggles and rebellions. By 1861 the country's finances were so bad that the nation owed 80 million pesos in foreign debts. Mexico's president, Benito Juarez, pledged to pay off these debts eventually but, as an emergency measure, he suspended all payment for two years.

In France, Napoleon III saw this as an opportunity to establish French colonies in Latin America. He believed that the United States was too involved with the Civil War to try and enforce the Monroe Doctrine, and that if the South won the war—and after the Battle of Bull Run it looked like they might—opposition to his plan would be minimal.

Napoleon enlisted England and Spain to join him in a mission to encourage Mexico to pay off its foreign debts. The mission began with the landing of French, English and Spanish troops at Vera Cruz. The French minister then demanded that Mexico pay 12 million pesos to France, an impossible amount, given the state of the Mexican treasury.

Napoleon then set up a provisional government with his personal emissary as its head, and brought in a much larger French army to enforce it. England and Spain, now realizing Napoleon's scheme for French domination, protested France's moves and withdrew their forces.

The French, now alone, marched 6000 dragoons and foot soldiers to occupy Mexico City. On May 5 (Cinco de Mayo), 1862, on their way to the capital, the French soldiers entered the town of Puebla. To stop the French, the Mexicans garrisoned a ragtag army of 4000 men at Puebla, most of them armed with fifty-year-old antiquated guns. The French general, contemptuous of the Mexicans, ordered his men to charge right into the center of the Mexican defenses.

The handsomely uniformed French cavalry charged through soggy ditches, over crumbling adobe walls, and up the steep slopes of the Cerro de Guadalupe, right into the Mexican guns. When the shooting was over, the French ended up with a thousand dead troops. The Mexicans then counterattacked and drove the French all the way to the coast.

Now the honor of France was at stake. Napoleon III committed an additional 28,000 men to the struggle. They eventually took over Puebla and Mexico City. Napoleon next arranged for the young archduke Maximilian, brother of Austria's Emperor Franz Joseph, to establish himself as emperor of Mexico, as a way to set up a legitimate-seeming government, while insuring French interests in Mexico. Maximilian's reign lasted just three years. On June 19, 1867, he was executed by a firing squad, four months after the last French troops left the country.

Every 5th of May in Mexico, school children throughout the country celebrate the victory of the Mexican people over the French at the Battle of Puebla, but these celebrations are minor compared to their counterparts in the United States, where millions of Americans drink beer, eat tacos and hold parties to celebrate Cinco de Mayo, even though they have no idea what the holiday is all about.

A young Tarahumara girl displays crafts to tourists at Divisadero. The sale of their homemade baskets, dolls, pottery and musical instruments provide the Indians with cash to purchase the supplies which they cannot produce themselves.

Copper Canyon Crafts

Visitors to the Copper Canyon area are always pleasantly surprised by the wide variety of craftsware and folk art available for purchase. The remote life and character of the Tarahumara Indians has fostered a tradition of crafts making as a part of their lifestyle.

While traveling through the region you will find very inexpensively priced baskets, belts, dolls, pottery and musical instruments.

The baskets are made out of the leaves of the agave as well as pine needles and range in size from tiny to large. Visitors purchasing baskets find that they can pack them one inside the other to conserve space during their trip. Once at home, the baskets of pine needles hold their scent of pine forests and become a wonderful reminder of the trip, and they are utilitarian as well as beautiful. The Tarahumara pottery is quite sturdy and is designed to be more functional then decorative.

Music is an important part of the Indians daily living and also plays an important roll in their ceremonies and festivals. Their musical instruments include violins, drums and wooden flutes. They learned the art of violin making from the Spaniards in the 18th century.

Carved wooden dolls dressed in typical Tarahumara fashion are for sale in a variety of sizes and portray the various activities of Tarahumara life—mothers wearing shawls while carrying babies on their backs, ladies weaving on hand-looms, and men carrying tools or musical instruments and wearing their traditional headgear.

Crafts can be purchased from the Indians who set up their merchandise on rocks along the trails and in all sorts of unlikely nooks and crannies. Crafts are also available in stores, and one that we recommend is the Mission Store in Creel, located right on the town square. Profits go to the hospital which serves the Tarahumara .

A Crested Caracara rests on a tree branch in Copper Canyon. More than 270 species of birds can be found in this region which spans four distinct biotic communities, ranging from sub-tropical, in the canyon bottoms, to Madrean Conifer Forests, on the canyon rims.

Copper Canyon is for the Birds

By Chuck Rau

Less than 300 miles below the U.S. border lie some of the most rugged and remote areas of northwestern Mexico—the region known as Copper Canyon.

This part of Mexico has some of the most varied habitats in North America, from the Madrean Conifer Forests at 8,000 feet on the canyon rims to sub-tropical areas in the canyon bottoms. With four distinctly different Biotic communities there is a wide diversity of flora and fauna. This is especially true with respect to bird life.

California Native trips through Copper Canyon travel through all four Biotic communities and participants see a great variety of birds. There are at least 270 species found in the region, many of which cannot be found in the United States.

Traveling on the Copper Canyon train you can see Black-throated Magpie Jays, Mourning and White-winged Doves, and Vermilion Flycatchers. On the tops of the Organ Pipe cactus perch Black vultures, with their wings outstretched to catch the warming rays of the rising sun, and Crested Caracaras.

At Divisadero, "The Viewpoint", where a breathtaking view overlooks the deepest part of the canyon, Barn Swallows, White-throated and Black Swifts soar over the canyon rim and walks through the surrounding woodlands turn up exciting birds like Blue-throated and Magnificent hummingbirds, Zone-tailed Hawks, and Hairy Woodpeckers. One time we watched a flock of about a dozen rare and endangered Thick-billed parrots fly by just below the rim of the canyon, right in front of our hotel.

At Lake Arareco, not far from the small town of Creel, are various types of waterfowl including Buffleheads, Ring-necked ducks, Blue-winged teals and even an occasional Osprey. A hike to Cusarare Falls brings sightings of Mexican Chickadees, Red-Faced Warblers, Brown Creepers, White-eared Hummingbirds, Dippers, Belted Kingfishers and the rare and elusive Eared Trogon, probably the most beautiful bird of the area.

In the semitropical habitat at the bottom of the canyon, at Batopilas, an entirely different array of birds can be seen. Broad-billed, Berylline, Violet-crowned and Lucifer hummingbirds frequent the many flowers. In the fruit trees are Orioles and Tanagers. Along the riverside Riparian areas there is always the chance to see White-fronted and Lilac-crowned Parrots and Elegant Trogons.

One time while visiting the ancient Cathedral at Satevo, 3 miles down river from Batopilas, I looked up to see three Military Macaws flying near by. These large beautiful green and blue parrots are at the most northern part of their range and seeing them is a memorable experience.

With its close proximity to the U.S. and unique blending of varied habitats, Copper Canyon affords a great opportunity to see many unique bird species while at the same time enjoying the spectacular scenery of the Sierra Madres.

The skies above Copper Canyon are spectacular but seldom as breathtaking as they were in the spring of 1997 when the comet Hale-Bopp traveled across the heavens.

Stargazing in the Canyon

By Chuck Rau

Deep, spectacular canyons, breathtaking vistas, remote mountain villages and the cave-dwelling Tarahumara Indians—these are all great reasons to join us on our Copper Canyon adventures. But in this remote area of Mexico's Sierra Madres the sky itself adds another incentive for making the journey.

Far from the lights of cities, the Sierra Madre nights are clear and dark. Looking skyward, you can see wondrous sights—meteorites, planets, stars and, on special occasions, some of the heavens' most spectacular exhibitions.

In spring of 1997 our Copper Canyon trips provided us perfect sites for viewing the comet Hale-Bopp, called the comet of the century. From vantage points along the canyon rim at Divisadero and Tejaban, and from the bottom of the canyon in the little town of Batopilas, we enjoyed spectacular views of this celestial visitor. One night after dinner we gathered outside of our hotel to view the comet at its closest approach. Many local citizens stopped to join us, and we ended up having an impromptu comet party in the remote mountain village of Creel.

Back in May of 1994 there was a near total eclipse of the sun. As our small group assembled along the canyon rim, I passed out the special glasses which I brought for viewing the eclipse. As the light began to fade, the local Tarahumara Indians came rushing to see what was happening to the sun, and together we all watched this unforgettable event.

What other astronomical shows will we be treated to on future Copper Canyon trips? Another eclipse, another comet, a meteor shower, E.T. or ...?

California Native Operations Manager, Laurie Kraft, shares Polaroid photo with young Tarahumara girl.

Kòrima

Kòrima, in the language of Copper Canyon's Tarahumara Indians, means *sharing*. Living in small family groups, the Tarahumara have been able to subsist in harmony with their environment by growing corn, beans, and squash on the plateaus and flood planes scattered throughout the deep canyons of their rugged homeland. Sharing and cooperation are an integral part of their lives. If one person has something for which another has greater need, then it is expected that it will be shared.

In 1992 and again in 1995, severe droughts caused near total failure of crops in a number of Tarahumara communities. Not only was the well being of the people threatened, but also their ability to maintain their traditional lifestyle.

Two of our longtime guides, Doug Stewart and Lynn Reinecke, conceived the Kòrima Food Projects to help the Indians get through these difficult periods.

Doug and Lynn began the original project by buying crafts from the

Tarahumaras and selling them in local shops in California. With the money raised and additional donations, they returned to the area with over 5 metric tons of food. Through a series of organized foot races and craft trades, the Tarahumaras were able to purchase needed food at a reasonable "price." The sale of these crafts purchased from the Indians was then used to buy additional food. More than six metric tons of food was delivered in April of 1993 to 180 Tarahumara families in eight different communities. A portion of the food was traded to the Indians for crafts. All of the money from the sales of these crafts were used to buy more food which was delivered to the Indians in July of that year. In total, more than eight metric tons of food was delivered to the Tarahumaras.

The goal of the project has always been to furnish aid to the people while not taking on the form of a charitable "give away." The production and sale of the crafts in exchange for food allows the people to maintain their dignity.

Besides the "Kòrima Food Project," Doug has been working closely with Tarahumara woodcarvers. In their delicate and finely worked violins, flutes and pine racing balls, the Tarahumara craftsmen exhibit great skill. Doug is a skilled wood-carver himself, and he noticed that the Tarahumaras were laboring with inferior tools, including discarded Mexican pocket knifes, old nails and glass. He felt that with better and more modern woodworking tools, the Indians could ease their work, increase production, and make a living while still preserving their age old cultural structure.

Since the beginning of this project, Doug has provided many Tarahumara artisans with high quality knives and other woodworking tools. Over the years, he has spent time in the home of a skilled violin maker and was thrilled to see the difference the new tools made. His future plans include the setting up of a community wood shop in a local Tarahumara community.

In October 1994, anthropologists Susan Smith and Rebecca Hahn along with California Native guides Lori Klein, Doug Stewart, and Lynn Reinecke delivered treadle sewing machines, materials, and training, to four remote Tarahumara communities.

Tarahumara women have traditionally been the caretakers of children and the home. For many years they have been supplementing the family income by producing crafts, such as handcrafted pine needle baskets and carved wooden dolls, clothed in traditional Tarahumara styles. To better their standard of living they are cautiously accepting Western resources that will help them increase production while still maintaining their cultural values. The sewing machines shorten the time it takes for them to produce their crafts and traditional clothing for sale to tourists. The project was funded by a grant from the Ella Lyman Cabot Trust and private donations.

Susan and Rebecca first visited Copper Canyon in March of 1993, escorted by California Native guide Lori Klein, herself an anthropologist, where they produced a video documentary for public television.

The winter of 1994 found Doug and Lynn playing the role of "Yankee Traders" in the small Indian village of Samachique on a dark and stormy night. They had stopped to seek shelter at the home of a family of Tarahumaras when the lady of the house asked if they had some cloth to trade. Doug, remembering the 35 yards of fabric they had brought as gifts, replied "Karaho","Yes" in Tarahumara. In no time at all they were surrounded by people wanting to barter. Lynn recalls the scene as something out of "Little House on the Prairie" when all of the town's women simultaneously tried to trade with the newly arrived peddler.

We are proud of Lynn, Doug, Lori, and the rest of our guides and we know that our guests appreciate the opportunity to travel with these dedicated people who spend so much of their free time making friends with the Tarahumara and teaching visitors to appreciate and respect their traditional culture.

A Tarahumara farmer tills his fields, using a horse-drawn plow, in much the same way as his ancestors have done for centuries. California Native guides Doug Stewart and Lynn Reinecke initiated a program to enrich the variety of crops grown by the Tarahumara.

Seeds of Friendship

By Doug Stewart

One of the things I love about being a guide in Copper Canyon is my friendship with the Tarahumara Indians. The Tarahumara are shy towards outsiders, but once they see that a person keeps returning, is interested in them, and treats them with respect, they open up.

The Tarahumaras are farmers who subsist in harmony with their environment by growing corn, beans, squash, and a few other staples on the plateaus and flood plains scattered throughout the deep canyons. I, having worked in agriculture for many years, share a common interest with them in making things grow.

One winter Lynn, my partner in all things, and I bought a case of a very good and unusual winter squash. As a long time gardener, it was my natural impulse to save the seed from these squash and to share it with my Tarahumara friends. The Indians planted the seed and were very happy with the results. They enthusiastically told me how big and delicious the squash were and how well they grew.

This experience led me to research other unique vegetable varieties that would be suitable for growing in the area. I contacted many seed companies and they were all very helpful and generous.

In order to be meaningful to the Tarahumara, the varieties need to be open-pollinated so that the seed saved for the next year's planting will stay true to the parent plant. They must also be new and unique to the Indians so as not to replace the adapted and proven varieties they already grow. My goal is to enhance, not to replace, the gene-pool of their food crops.

It would be a disservice to the Tarahumaras to give them seed that is not suitable for their growing conditions. It is already hard for them to grow enough food to feed their families without wasting their time in growing plants that don't do well.

All in all, it has been a rewarding experience, furthering my friendship with these people, and, I hope, sharing some of my blessings with them.

The route from Chihuahua City to El Paso was once part of "El Camino Real de Tierra Adentro" (the Royal Road of Interior Land) which connected with the Santa Fe trail to bring millions of dollars worth of goods from Independence, Missouri, to Mexico.

The Way to Santa Fe

By Don Fuchik

Thousands of traders and homesteaders followed the Santa Fe Trail from Independence, Missouri to Santa Fe, New Mexico, transporting millions of dollars in goods. But the goods did not stay in Santa Fe. Most were moved south over *El Camino Real de Tierra Adentro* (The Royal Road of Interior Land) to Chihuahua City and central Mexico. The Santa Fe Trail probably would not have existed without the Camino Real.

This ancient route dates back to prehistoric times when Indians from the Aztec capital at Tenochtitlan, now Mexico City, followed this route to northwestern Chihuahua. By 1540, Spanish miners, traders, missionaries, soldiers and cattle drovers moved northward along the Camino Real.

In 1598, the conquistador, Juan de Oñate, followed this route, leading the first permanent European settlers into what is now the United States. By 1609, the road ran from Mexico City to Santa Fe, carrying trade items and new settlers.

In addition to being an immigration and trade route, the Camino Real was also an invasion route. During the war between the United States and Mexico, Colonel Alexander W. Doniphan led a small force of volunteers from Missouri to capture Chihuahua City. At the Sacramento River, just outside of Chihuahua City, this force defeated a much larger Mexican unit. The battle site is marked by a monolith clearly visible from our bus at the first toll booth out of Ciudad Chihuahua.

Doniphan's regiment occupied the city the next day, but evacuated it shortly thereafter in order to join a larger American force to the east. His group had then completed a march of well over 3,000 miles through some of the worst weather and terrain conditions imaginable.

Trade continued after the war and a railroad was built linking El Paso with Mexico City. Today, traveling along this route from Chihuahua to El Paso, we see an occasional freight train, but there is no longer passenger service. The Chihuahua al Pacifico Railroad, the famous Copper Canyon train, is one of the few passenger services left in Mexico today.

One of my favorite times in leading groups through Copper Canyon is this last day of our trip where we follow this historic route from Chihuahua to El Paso. As our bus follows Mexican Highway 45, the travelers reminisce about the wonderful experiences we have shared. The country is flat and arid, so different from the rugged mountains and canyons of the Sierra Madres which we have left behind us.

We pass few settlements along the way. El Sueco, named to honor a Swedish settler who came here many years ago, and Villa Ahumada, named for a general in the Mexican Revolution. We cross the border and travel to the El Paso Airport, bidding farewell to our friends and to our Copper Canyon journey.

At the Tarahumara settlement of Kirare, on the route to Batopilas, a man and woman prepare their evening meal. The Tarahumara lifestyle has changed little over the past several hundred years.

Time Traveler

By Doug Stewart

I feel as if I have been transported back into time. I am sitting on the floor of a cave in the side of a rocky canyon wall, at the bottom of Copper Canyon, sharing a meal of beans and tortillas with a Tarahumara family, who appear to be Indians right out of the old west.

"How did I get here?" I ask myself.

I love being in nature, hiking and backpacking, and have always been fascinated by the life styles of the Indians. So it was natural that once I discovered Copper Canyon, with its Tarahumara Indians living their age old lifestyle, that I wanted to keep coming back.

Over the years I have returned, time and again, to these beautiful mountains, made friends with the Tarahumara people, and worked with them on many projects. For years now, I have led California Native trips into this area and I enjoy introducing visitors to the Tarahumara and giving them the chance to appreciate the unique customs and lifestyle of these wonderful people.

When I am in these isolated canyons with the Tarahumara time seems to stop. It is if I had traveled back to a very different, valuable, and ancient world.

On these worn paths, leading up and down the steep canyons of the Sierra Madres, I feel happy and fulfilled, and consider myself to be a very fortunate *Time Traveler*.

Appendix

Lori's Tips for Trips

By Lori Klein

Packing:

What's the most difficult part of going on a trip? Planning? Air tickets? Hotels? The thing which I find hardest is packing. I hate it! But like the rest of you, I love traveling and must face this formidable task. These hints can make your trip preparations less painful.

1. Pack Light. No matter where they're going or for how long, many people believe they can't survive without the kitchen sink. If you can't carry it, don't take it!

2. Limit changes of clothes. Why worry about matching color schemes? Limit yourself and concentrate on the real purpose of the trip—Having fun!

3. Forget the appliances. Don't weigh down your bag with an electric razor, hair dryer or radio? You're on vacation. Let your hair down.

4. Prepare for the unexpected. Layers work best. If the weather changes you can put it on or take it off.

5. Think twice. Go for clothes that serve a dual purpose such as a waterproof jacket that can also be worn on an evening out.

6. Don't fold, roll. This is definitely the most compact and best way to keep your clothes from getting wrinkled.

7. Save your favorites for home. If you can't bear to lose it, don't bring it.

8. Keep the essentials close at hand. Never pack away travelers checks, passport, tickets or any other important documents. A small day pack holds a number of things and can easily be slung over your shoulder.

9. Take time. Packing a little in advance gives you time to rest and a chance to make last minute changes.

10. Always pack the basic skin protectors. Chapstick, hand lotion, bug repellent and sun screen can make your trip more comfortable.

11. Prescription drugs. If you take a prescription drug, bring an adequate supply for your trip and a copy of your prescription.

Communicate:

I lead many trips to Mexico and all of my groups have a wonderful time, but some people wish that they could communicate better with the locals. From my own experience, I've discovered that the "locals" appreciate any effort you make to communicate. As much as you want to know about them, they also want to know about you. Even if you never plan on becoming fluent in Spanish, there are ways to communicate, and these few hints can help you break down the communication barrier.

1. Take a language class at your local adult school or community college.

2. Bring along a small phrase book.

3. Try charades—an ancient but useful form of communication.

4. Bring along pictures of your family and home. These are great icebreakers.

While Traveling:

Traveling is enjoyable, but we sometimes have to spend hours hanging around at airports or train stations. These tips can help pass the time and give you a little more comfort.

1. Take advantage of non-moving restrooms. The restrooms in any depot have a lot more space and breathing room than those on a train or plane.

2. Catch up on the news. Relax with a local paper.

3. Say hello to someone you don't know. People on the go have a number of missions and goals. You could find yourself involved in a fascinating conversation, perhaps making a new friend in the process.

4. Walk instead of ride. Movable walkways may be convenient, but if you've been sitting for several hours, leg exercise can really help.

5. Freshen up. Carry a small toothbrush, comb, washcloth or other personal items in your hand luggage.

6. Watch your posture. Sitting or sleeping for any length of time in the wrong position can put a strain on your neck and lower back. Try some simple stretches.

Be Comfortable:

Traveling can be wonderful, exciting, and fun. However, when we become uncomfortable, we tend to become unhappy. To make your trips as enjoyable as possible, try the following.

1. Carry a small, inflatable pillow. They fit easily into hand luggage and can be pulled out anywhere.

2. While traveling, choose water or juice. Alcohol and caffeinated beverages act as diuretics and dehydrators.

3. Get a good night's sleep before a long journey. Travel can be exhausting, especially when changing time zones.

4. Wear loose fitting clothes. Clothing should not bind or restrict, be versatile, and allow maximum comfort.

5. Bring along a few snacks. Even a piece of gum or hard candy can curb a hunger pang.

Traveling in Mexico:

These hints that can make your travels south of the border mas facil (easier) and divertido (fun).

1. Cross the communication barrier. People will be a lot more helpful and friendly towards the visitor who makes even the most basic effort to communicate. Even a simple *"Hola!"* (Hi) and smile will get you a long way.

2. Appropriate dress works best. Because dress styles vary within each culture, visitors may find themselves in the uncomfortable position of wearing attire that's too revealing or casual. Dress comfortably but practice good-judgment.

3. Let your palate explore. Part of the fun of traveling is sampling the local cuisine. Don't turn your nose in the air when offered something new. You might be in for a pleasant surprise.

4. Leave stereotypes behind. All people have preconceived notions about unfamiliar places and new people. Mexico, like the United States, has a very diversified population.

5. Money, money, money. It is not necessary to change large quantities of dollars before leaving home, but it's always nice to arrive with something in your pocket. Smaller denominations work best and are easier to change. Travelers checks can be difficult to cash in remote areas.

6. Do a little homework. Reading up on Mexico and learning something about its history, geography and culture can make your trip more fun and interesting.

Memories:

Make your trip last a lifetime—or at least the memories. It's fun and oh-so-easy to make a memory book. Here's all you'll need to get started:

1. A blank book—hard or soft cover will work.

2. A glue stick, highlighter, pair of scissors—use these to paste in receipts, magazine and newspaper clippings and other interesting things that will help you remember fun spots, hotels and restaurants.

3. A pen or two—to jot down the names of special places you visited and special people you met. Don't forget unusual plants and animals you saw.

4. A pencil/colored pencils—try your hand at drawing, even if you're not an artist. It's fun to be creative.

Trees and Plants of Copper Canyon

Compiled by Charles S. Rau

Sinaloan Thorn Scrub

Elevation: Sea Level to 500 feet
Average Rainfall: 16 inches/year

Blue Palo Verde
Elephant Tree (Torote)
Hecho Cactus
Kapok
Mexican Little leaf Palo Verde
Mexican Mesquite
Organpipe Cactus
Prickly Pear Cactus (Nopal)
Queen's Wreath
Redbird of Paradise
San Miguelito
Sea Grape
Tree Morning Glory
Tree Ocotillo
Whitethorn Acacia
Yellow Thumpetbush

Sinaloan Deciduous Thorn Forest

Elevation: 900 to 3,500 feet
Average Rainfall: 8 inches/year

Amate Prieta Fig
Goldman Fig
Gumbo Limbo
Hecho Cactus
Kapock
Montezuma Cypress
Octopus Agave
Orate Cane Bamboo
Pink Amapa
Rock Fig
Sabal Palm
Tree Coral Bean
Tree Morning Glory

Madrean Evergreen Woodland

Elevation: 4,000 to 7,300 feet
Average Rainfall: 20-22 inches/year

Alligator bark Juniper
Apache Pine
Arizona Cypress
Arizona Madrone
Arizona White Oak
Chihuahua Pine
Durango Pine
Hand Basin Oak
Mexican Blue Oak
Mexican Pinyon Pine
Mountain Alder
Netleaf Oak
Pointleaf Manzanita
Silver Leaf Oak
Texas Madrone
Weeping or Sad Pine

Madrean Conifer Forest

Elevation: 7,000 to 9,000 feet
Average Rainfall: 28 inches/year

Alligator bark Juniper
Arizona Cypress
Arizona White Oak
Bracken Fern
Chihuahua Pine
Douglas Fir
Durango Pine
Englemann Spruce
Few-leaved Goldenrod
Mexican White Pine
Mountain Alder
Netleaf Oak
Quaking Aspen
Thick-leaf Oak
Weeping Pine
Wild Strawberry

Birds of Copper Canyon

Compiled by Charles S. Rau

1. Great Egret **O**
2. Snowy Egret **O**
3. Cattle Egret **C**
4. Green-backed Heron **O**
5. Black-crowned Night Heron **R**
6. Green-winged Teal **C**
7. Mallard **C**
8. Blue-winged Teal **C**
9. Bufflehead **R**
10. Black Vulture **C**
11. Turkey Vulture **C**
12. Osprey **R**
13. Northern Harrier **O**
14. Sharp-shinned Hawk **C**
15. Cooper's Hawk **O**
16. Northern Goshawk **O**
17. Common Black Hawk **O**
18. Harris' Hawk **O**
19. Gray Hawk **O**
20. Short-tailed Hawk **R**
21. Swainson's Hawk **R**
22. Zone-tailed Hawk **C**
23. Red-tailed Hawk **C**
24. Crested Caracara **C**
25. Laughing Falcon **R**
26. American Kestrel **C**
27. Bat Falcon **R**
28. Wild Turkey **R**
29. Montezuma Quail **O**
30. Elegant Quail **O**
31. Gambel's Quail **C**
32. American Coot **C**
33. Black-bellied Plover **C**
34. Snowy Plover **O**
35. Wilson's Plover **C**
36. Killdeer **C**
37. Wilson's Phalarope **C**
38. Red-necked Phalarope **C**
39. Rock Dove **C**
40. Band-tailed Pigeon **O**
41. White-winged Dove **C**
42. Mourning Dove **C**
43. Inca Dove **C**
44. Common Ground Dove **C**
45. Ruddy Ground Dove **R**
46. White-tipped Dove **O**
47. Green Parakeet **O**
48. Military Macaw **O**
49. Thick-billed Parrot **R**
50. Blue-rumped Parrolet **C**
51. White-fronted Parrot **O**
52. Lilac-crowned Parrot **O**
53. Yellow-billed Cuckoo **O**
54. Squirrel Cuckoo **O**
55. Greater Roadrunner **C**
56. Groove-billed Ani **C**
57. Barn Owl **C**
58. Western Screech Owl **C**
59. Great Horned Owl **C**
60. Northern Pygmy Owl **O**
61. Ferruginous Pygmy-Owl **O**
62. Elf Owl **O**
63. Burrowing Owl **O**
64. Lesser Nighthawk **C**
65. Common Poorwill **O**
66. Whip-poor-will **C**
67. Black Swift **O**
68. Chestnut-collard Swift **O**
69. White-throated Swift **C**
70. Broad-billed Hummingbird **C**
71. White-eared Hummingbird **C**
72. Berylline Hummingbird **C**
73. Violet-crowned Hummingbird **C**
74. Blue-throated Hummingbird **C**
75. Magnificent Hummingbird **O**
76. Plain-capped Starthroat **O**
77. Black-chinned Hummingbird **O**
78. Costa's Hummingbird **R**
79. Broad-tailed Hummingbird **O**
80. Rufous Hummingbird **O**
81. Allen's Hummingbird **O**
82. Mountain Trogon **O**
83. Elegant Trogon **C**
84. Eared Trogon **C**
85. Belted Kingfisher **C**
86. Green Kingfisher **O**
87. Acorn Woodpecker **C**
88. Gila Woodpecker **C**
89. Red-naped Sapsucker **C**
90. Williamson's Sapsucker **O**
91. Ladder-backed Woodpecker **C**
92. Hairy Woodpecker **O**
93. Strickland's Woodpecker **R**
94. Northern Flicker **C**
95. Red-shafted Flicker **C**
96. Northern Beardless Tyrannulet **O**
97. Tufted Flycatcher **O**
98. Greater Pewee **C**
99. Western Wood Pewee **R**
100. Willow Flycatcher **O**
101. Hammond's Flycatcher **C**
102. Dusky Flycatcher **C**
103. Gray Flycatcher **C**
104. Black Phoebe **C**
105. Vermilion Flycatcher **C**
106. Dusky-capped Flycatcher **C**
107. Ash-throated Flycatcher **C**
108. Brown-crested Flycatcher **O**
109. Great Kiskadee **C**
110. Sulphur-bellied Flycatcher **C**
111. Cassin's Kingbird **C**
112. Thick-billed Kingbird **O**
113. Western Kingbird **C**
114. Violet-green Swallow **C**

115. Cliff Swallow **C**
116. Barn Swallow **C**
117. Steller's Jay **C**
118. Black-throated Magpie Jay **C**
119. Scrub Jay **O**
120. Mexican Jay **C**
121. Mexican (Sinaloan) Crow **C**
122. Common Raven **C**
123. Chihuahuan Raven **C**
124. Mexican Chickadee **C**
125. Bridled Titmouse **C**
126. Bushtit **O**
127. White-breasted Nuthatch **C**
128. Pygmy Nuthatch **R**
129. Brown Creeper **C**
130. Cactus Wren **C**
131. Rock Wren **C**
132. Canyon Wren **C**
133. Sinaloa Wren **O**
134. Happy Wren **O**
135. Bewick's Wren **C**
136. House Wren **C**
137. Ruby-crowned Kinglet **C**
138. Black-capped Gnatcatcher **O**
139. Eastern Bluebird **O**
140. Western Bluebird **C**
141. Mountain Bluebird **O**
142. Townsend's Solitaire **O**
143. Rufous-backed Robin **O**
144. American Robin **C**
145. Bendire's Thrasher **O**
146. Curve-billed Thrasher **C**
147. Cedar Waxwing **R**
148. Gray Silky-flycatcher **O**
149. Phainopepla **O**
150. Loggerhead Shrike **C**
151. Bell's Vireo **C**
152. Black-capped Vireo **O**

153. Solitary Vireo **O**
154. Hutton's Vireo **R**
155. Warbling Vireo **C**
156. Orange-crowned Warbler **C**
157. Nashville Warbler **C**
158. Virginia's Warbler **O**
159. Lucy's Warbler **C**
160. Yellow-rumped Warbler **C**
161. Black-throated Gray Warbler **C**
162. Townsend's Warbler **C**
163. Palm Warbler **O**
164. Prothonotary Warbler **O**
165. MacGillivary's Warbler **O**
166. Common Yellowthroat **C**
167. Wilson's Warbler **C**
168. Red-faced Warbler **O**
169. Painted Redstart **C**
170. Slate-throated Redstart **O**
171. Rufous-capped Warbler **O**
172. Blue-hooded Euphonia **O**
173. Hepatic Tanager **C**
174. Western Tanager **C**
175. Flame-colored Tanager **R**
176. Red-headed Tanager **O**
177. Northern Cardinal **C**
178. Pyrrhuloxia **C**
179. Yellow Grosbeak **O**
180. Black-headed Grosbeak **C**
181. Blue Grosbeak **C**
182. Lazuli Bunting **O**
183. Indigo Bunting **O**
184. Varied Bunting **O**
185. Green-tailed Towhee **C**
186. Rufous-sided Towhee **C**
187. Brown Towhee **C**
188. Rufous-crowned Sparrow **O**
189. Rusty Sparrow **O**
190. Striped Sparrow **O**

191. Chipping Sparrow **C**
192. Brewer's Sparrow **C**
193. Black-chinned Sparrow **R**
194. Vesper Sparrow **C**
195. Lark Sparrow **C**
196. Black-throated Sparrow **O**
197. Song Sparrow **C**
198. Lincoln's Sparrow **C**
199. White-throated Sparrow **O**
200. White-crowned Sparrow **C**
201. Dark-eyed Junco **C**
202. Yellow-eyed Junco **C**
208. Red-winged Blackbird **C**
204. Eastern Meadowlark **C**
205. Western Meadowlark **C**
206. Yellowheaded Blackbird **O**
207. Great-tailed Grackle **C**
208. Bronzed Cowbird **C**
209. Brown-headed Cowbird **C**
210. Hooded Oriole **C**
211. Streaked-back Oriole **O**
212. Northern Oriole **C**
213. Scott's Oriole **O**
214. Purple Finch **C**
215. House Finch **C**
216. Red Crossbill **O**
217. Pine Siskin **C**
218. Lesser Goldfinch **C**
219. Lawrence's Goldfinch **O**
220. Evening Grosbeak **O**
221. House Sparrow **C**

C - Common (seen every year)
O - Occasional (seen occasionally)
R - Rare (seen sporadically or rarely)

Guide to the Government Palace Murals

By Chihuahua State Government, Ministry of Commercial and Tourist Development

On the patio walls of the State Government Building are the murals painted by Aaron Piña Mora, during Teofilo Borunda's government period (1956-1962); where Chihuahua's history from the 16th century to the Mexican Revolution is represented.

This building was under construction from 1881 until 1892, but was destroyed by a fire in 1941 When reconstruction began, it was decided that another floor should be added.

Following is a brief explanation of what Aaron Piña Mora wishes to represent in each of his murals, starting at the entrance and continuing clockwise, to the left.

1. The first mural represents the first Europeans that set foot in our territory: Alvaro Nuñez Cabeza de Vaca, Andres Durantes, Alonso del Castillo and Estebanico, a mulatto slave. Estebanico was fast at learning American languages and Cabeza de Vaca would pose as a shaman or medicine man and would get presents from the natives. Instead of using exorcisms or potions, he would pronounce passages from the bible, using two sticks to form a cross.

2. The next mural shows the explorers at the mining estates. The first one is Santa Barbola, now known as Santa Barbara. Francisco de Ibarra is the man on horseback. We can also see Cristobal de Ontiveros, who brought cattle to our state, which, to this day, continues to be one the main economic activities.

3. In this mural we see the arrival of the first settlers and missionaries who introduced Catholicism to Chihuahua. The settler's goal was to exploit the recently found mines. The natives were treated abominably and even made into slaves. This situation continued, for the next 250 years, and though things have improved greatly, serious inequalities still exist.

4. Teporaca, known for his prowess with the axe, was the last leader of the Tarahumaran rebellion. He was hanged on March 4th, 1653.

5. The following mural represents the natives' struggle for freedom. The newly found gold and silver mines attracted more and more settlers seeking riches. This mural depicts how the City of Chihuahua's economy depended on the Santa Eulalia mine. In order to decide where the city (Real de Minas) was going to be founded, a vote was taken. It was a tie, so Governor Antonio de Deza y Ulloa voted for the place where the Sacramento and Chuviscar rivers meet, instead of Santa Eulalia. That is how the City of Chihuahua was founded on October 12, 1709 under the name Real de Minas de san Francisco de Cuellar. This painting represents the most important moment in the life of our city. The two bottom panels represent agriculture and mining, on which the economy was based in the 18th century.

6. The 200 years of Apache domination are represented in this mural. This was a dramatic time fraught by constant war between the settlers and the nomads, until the Apaches surrendered in 1883. The bottom mural shows the construction of the Cathedral in 1725. The church had to satisfy all the needs of the people who lived in San Felipe el Real, and was built with donations from miners and businessmen.

7. On the bottom panel of this same mural we see the war techniques used by the Apaches. The shaman gets all the tribe chiefs together and gives them each a narrow strip of suede with 11 knots. During the trip back to their tribes, each chief cuts off one knot every night. The last knot marked the night before the orchestrated Apache attack on the Spanish jails.

8. In this mural we see the arrival of Don Miguel Hidalgo y Costilla to our city, accompanied by other Independence leaders (Aldama, Abasolo, Allende and Jimenez), after being captured in 1811 to be judged and sentenced.

9. Here we can see the proclamation that was published when Miguel Hidalgo, the Father of our Country, arrived in Chihuahua. This document prohibited all from cheering or applauding "the traitor," who was sentenced and executed here in Chihuahua.

10. The next mural represents the northerners protesting against Spanish oppression, which was considered one of the first outbursts of the future Independence War.

11. This allegory refers to Hidalgo's trial: he is stripped of his clergy title and handed over to the military authorities to be executed by firing-squad after being' imprisoned for 98 days in a dungeon. The bottom mural shows the interior of Hidalgo's dungeon and his personal belongings. The execution took place inside the Jesuit's school, which today is the State Government Building, on July 30, 1811 at 7:00 a.m.

12. "The shooting of the light" is the name of this mural, which portrays the expression on Miguel Hidalgo's face just before he was executed. Behind him we can see Ignacio Allende, Mariano Jimenez, Juan Aldama and Manuel Santa Maria, Who were some' of the most important rebels executed just days before Hidalgo. On the left you can see a priest destroying native idols; a landowner ignoring the law and treating his workers like slaves; people suffering, and, in the center, a rebel breaking the chains of slavery and swearing allegiance to the flag, symbol or our country.

13. The next mural is dedicated to the memory of Benito Juarez, who was the first president of our country. In this mural he is shown with two other freedom fighters: Abraham Lincoln and Simon Bolivar, and, in the background we find some of the most important reformers of our country. Justice represented by a sword whose light makes all men equal looms in the background. On the top left side are the local heroes who fought beside Juarez in the "Guerra de Reforma" against the French invaders and the Empire; they are: Gen. Esteban Coronado, Gen. Manuel Ojinaga and Gen. Luis Terrazas.

14. In 1823, the National Congress put an end to what was known as "Nueva Vizcaya" and gave birth to the provinces of Chihuahua and Durango. In 1825 the first printer's shop was opened in the state and the newspapers "La Espada", "La Adarga" and "el Centinela" are published.

15. First panel on the bottom: the liberal party is created to fight against Santana's dictatorship; in 1844 Gen. Angel Trias is named governor, and for the first time in local history a governor is democratically elected by the people.

16. First panel on top: between 1846 and 1847 the three most important battles in our state took place during the U.S. invasion: Temascalitos, Sacramento and Rosales. On the left we can see the main warriors from Chihuahua: Gen. Trias, Ignacio Irigoyen, Esteban Coronado and Jose Eligio Muñoz; in the center we see Agustin Melgar, who died at Chapultepec Castle in Mexico City.

17. The right side of the mural is dedicated to the memory of some of the most renowned men during the 1862 French invasion: Gen. Manuel Ojinaga, Gen. Luis Terrazas, Colonel Joaquin Terrazas and Pedro Meoqui.

18. Second panel on the bottom: Lieutenant General Alejo Garcia Conde, Jose Eligio Muñoz and Pedro Irigoyen represented our State at the Federal Congress in 1857, where our Constitution was written.

19. Third panel on the bottom: On August , 1858, a group of locals sign a document swearing to uphold the liberal Reform laws; Gen. Esteban Colorado was leader of the group.

20. Colonel Joaquin Terrazas and Juan Mata Ortiz are remembered as the heroes of the battle of "Tres Castillos," which took place in 1880. During this battle the Indian Vittorio was killed by Mauricio Corredor, and the conflict between the settlers and the nomads, which lasted 250 years, came to an end.

21. Fourth bottom panel: on March 2, 1876, the first telegraph was inaugurated in the state capital, and on April 23rd of that same year, communication was established between Rosales and Chihuahua. In 1883 the public service for Aldama was inaugurated. The 1882 Public Education Law established the following careers: grade school teacher, lawyer, notary and old people.

22. Fifth bottom panel: this mural represents the strike at Pinos Altos, the first attempt by the local workers to defend their rights. They demanded salaries to be paid in cash, instead of in vouchers they had to redeem at the landlords store. They were sentenced to death three days before the Chicago killings. On May 1, we celebrate Labor Day.

23. On the mural on the bottom right we can see the faces of those who helped paint these murals: Jose Carlos Chavez, Jose V. Escobar, Francisco R. Almada, Teofilo Borunda and Aaron Piña Mora.

24. When the political campaign for the federal elections of 1916 started in Chihuahua opposition against Porfirio Diaz was headed by Abraham Gonzalez who gained a large following in support of Francisco I. Madero, accompanied by Dolores Romero de Revilla, an anti-reelection feminist.

25. The next to the last mural is dedicated to Pascual Orozco, one of the most popular revolutionaries of 1910. His nakedness represents the purity of his beliefs, his thoughts, and his soul; he always helped his comrades in arms, destitute men and women. With him are those who fought by his side.

26. In the last mural we can see Francisco Villa, famous revolutionary and head of the Division del Norte. This painting shows his victory in Zacatecas over Huerta's army. Francisco Villa, whose real name was Doroteo Arango, contributed to the success of the Mexican Revolution.